The Sustainable Vegetable Garden:

A Backyard Guide to Healthy Soil and Higher Yields

The Sustainable Vegetable Garden:

A Backyard Guide to Healthy Soil and Higher Yields

John Jeavons

and

Carol Cox

Ecology Action

Illustrations by Sue Ellen Parkinson

TEN SPEED PRESS

Much of the data and other information in this book has been drawn from *How to Grow More Vegetables,* fifth ed., by John Jeavons, Ten Speed Press, 1995.

Ecology Action
5798 Ridgewood Road
Willits, CA 95490-9730
(707) 459-0150

Library of Congress Cataloging-in-Publication Data

Jeavons, John.
       The sustainable vegetable garden : a backyard guide to healthy soil and higher yields/
John Jeavons and Carol Cox ; illustrations by Sue Ellen Parkinson.
       p.   cm.
       Rev. ed. of: Lazy-bed gardening. c1993.
       Includes bibliographical references (p.) and index.
       ISBN 1-58008-016-2 (alk. paper)
       1. Vegetable gardening.   2. Biointensive gardening.   I. Cox, Carol.   II. Jeavons,
John. Lazy-bed gardening.   II. Title.
       SB324.3.J47   1999
       635-dc21   98-49296
                                                                          CIP

About the Boise Peace Quilters: On the cover of *The Sustainable Vegetable Garden* is a photo of Quilt #19, awarded to John Jeavons in 1988. The Peace Quilters use needle and thread to create their art in recognition of significant contributions toward bringing peace to the world. Quilts have been exchanged with peacemakers in many countries. Among the other recipients are Dr. Helen Caldicott, Pete Seeger, and Senator Frank Church. For more information about the Peace Quilters, send a self-addressed stamped envelope to BOISE PEACE QUILT PROJECT, P.O. Box 6469, Boise, ID 83707.

Cover design by Toni Tajima.
Interior design by Laura Lind.
Printed on recycled paper in the United States of America.
2 3 4 5 6 7 8 9 —03 02 01 00 99

To the gardeners of the Earth,

who are breathing life back into the soil

Contents

Acknowledgments

Special thanks to

• the people at Ten Speed Press—Phil Wood, publisher; Toni Goode, for cover design; Laura Lind, of Laura Lind Design, for book design; Wade Fox, for copy-editing; Jean Mann for proofreading and indexing; and Jason Rath, project editor, for his patience and persistence in asking incisive questions. Everyone assisted in so many ways so this book could be published at this time.

• Mary Campagna and Cynthia Raiser at Ecology Action for proofreading and editing suggestions; and

• our neighbors, Bill and JoAnn Kerrick, for graciously sharing their electricity and their upstairs bedroom for the three weeks it took to do the original typesetting.

Preface

More than twenty-five years ago, Ecology Action published the first best-selling how-to book on high-yield, resource-conserving, biologically intensive food-raising techniques. At the time little was known about these "new" sustainable Biointensive farming methods, which are actually thousands of years old. We spent several years rediscovering these exciting practices and then shared them in *How to Grow More Vegetables Than You Ever Thought Possible on Less Land Than You Can Imagine.* Over 350,000 copies are now in print in seven languages, plus Braille. Ecology Action currently has over thirty publications in use in 110 countries. Hundreds of other books and publications have drawn upon ours to include Biointensive techniques. Major regreening projects are underway in Mexico, Kenya, the Philippines, India, and Russia.

The original *How to Grow More Vegetables* was a relatively simple book, and as the years passed and we learned more, new editions were published by Ten Speed Press. Eventually, the thrust of the book became how to grow more food and emphasized the growing of calorie crops such as grains and beans, as well as fruits and nuts, herbs, flowers, and even fiber crops. In the process, the book became longer and a bit too technical for some, particularly beginning gardeners.

As a result, Ecology Action and Ten Speed Press decided that a simpler book should be written for those trying these methods for the first time, as well as for the seasoned gardener in need of streamlined information. *The Sustainable Vegetable Garden* is the result. This book is the distillation of over twenty years of our own experience and the experiences of thousands of other gardeners around the world. We are delighted to be able to share it with you. Some technical information has been included, which can be bypassed easily if you do not need that level of detail. We hope this book will make it easier for you to create "living soil" and a wonderful, lush, vibrant mini-ecosystem in your own backyard—or even your front yard—resulting in an edible landscape that will provide you with fresh and stored food all through the year.

John Jeavons • Willits, California • January 1, 1999

Introduction

Imagine yourself as a plant and think about where you would like to live. You cannot walk around and look for food and shelter; they must be within easy reach of your roots. As your roots and root hairs grow out in search of food, they will move more easily through loose, moist soil. You will grow strong and healthy if those roots find an ample supply of microscopic organisms ready and waiting to make nutrients available for your dining pleasure.

In sustainable gardening, the focus is on the soil. By creating and maintaining a living, healthy soil the gardener will be able to grow health-giving food. One good way to ensure sustainable soil fertility is the Biointensive method of food raising. This method, properly used, can be truly sustainable.

Biointensive food raising starts with a deeply prepared garden bed whose growing area, with its closely spaced plants, can produce up to four times more than an equivalent shallow bed planted in rows. This bed means less work for the gardener,

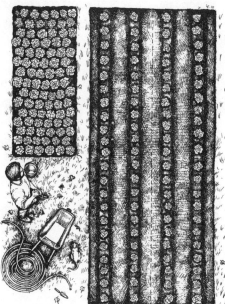

Biointensive fertility: four times the productivity in one-quarter the area!

Row, end view

with only one bed to dig, one bed to fertilize, one bed to water, and one bed to weed. And this bed uses only one quarter the area it would take to produce the same yield by other methods.

Its soil is

Biointensive bed, end view

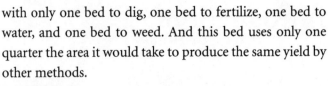

- loosened 2 feet deep, which results in lots of pore space for air, water, and roots;
- evenly moist because water can pass through it easily;
- full of nutrients and organic matter provided by compost;
- and planted with a variety of crops, closely spaced to provide a "living mulch," reflecting nature's diversity.

Because the soil is loosened so deep, the plant roots are able to penetrate further down into the soil, instead of needing to spread out in search of water and nutrients. For that reason, plants can be spaced more closely in a Biointensive bed, allowing more plants than in a garden plot using other soil preparation methods. Also, water is more readily available to plants because more of it is retained in the deeply loosened, compost-enriched soil.

LOOKING BACK TO NATURE

A Biointensive bed is not a modern invention. Before there were farmers and gardeners, nature kept the soil covered with a profusion of plants suited to their particular environment. Plants grew best where the soil was the richest, and they did not grow in rows.

Some of the earliest gardeners tried to mimic nature at its most productive. The Chinese began using biologically intensive—"biointensive"—raised beds in food production over 4,000 years ago. The Greeks realized 2,000 years ago that crops grew better in the loose soil of landslides.

Indigenous people in Central and South America as early as 2,000 years ago created extensive areas of large raised beds between irrigation channels. In the wet season, they planted their crops on the raised surfaces. During the dry season, when the raised fields were dried out, they planted in the irrigation channels to make use of the water stored within the soil.

In more recent times, the Irish developed their version of raised beds for planting potatoes. They called them "lazy beds" because they knew this method produced more food for their efforts.

Intensive raised-bed systems are a proven method for successfully raising large quantities of food, sustainably, over long periods. For a garden to be sustainable, food must be grown for the soil as well as for people. Fortunately, many of the best crops that produce food for the soil also produce food for people.

YOUR BIOINTENSIVE BED

The purpose of this book is to help you start your Biointensive garden. You will be introduced to a different way of looking at gardening, and you will learn to plan your crops, double-dig your bed, build your compost pile, and raise and transplant your seedlings.

The techniques are simple for getting started in a small, easy to maintain, and highly productive garden that can produce all the vegetables—and more—for your family, in a very small area.

Chapter 1 Thinking about Raising Food Sustainably

In a natural ecosystem, the fertility of the soil is maintained through the recycling of nutrients and the replenishment of organic matter. Only as much grows as the soil can support.

In our backyard gardens and on our farms, we interrupt the natural cycles and expect the soil to grow different kinds of plants. We often remove much of what the soil produces, eat it, and flush the nutrients away. We try to replenish the soil nutrients by purchasing fertilizers and compost. However, these products contain nutrients and organic matter produced by another area, usually without being replaced there.

The goal for a healthy ecosystem in a sustainable backyard garden is for the growing area to produce food while maintaining the fertility of the soil from within the garden itself.

Creating such an ecosystem is a way to participate in this living process. In addition, it can actually allow you to grow *all* of your nutrition in your backyard.

Many gardeners begin by raising tomatoes, cucumbers, onions, green beans, and lettuce in a small area. As the garden begins to flourish, potatoes, carrots, corn, and melons are often added. Once a garden is successful, other crops like dry beans and grains can be added to these favorite vegetables. Just as important, however, are crops that can be used to replenish the soil nutrients used up by these food crops.

COMPOST CROPS: A Key Approach to a Sustainable Garden

Growing plants need nourishment, just like children, and that plant nourishment is best obtained from a naturally healthy soil. Keeping the soil healthy means making sure it is balanced nutritionally. Whenever we harvest plants from a garden to eat or sell, we are taking nutrients from the soil. Making compost from all garden debris and kitchen waste and putting the compost in our garden beds means that some of the nutrients removed will be returned to the soil.

Compost Crop

A compost crop is a crop grown to provide material for the compost pile, especially at times when food crops are not being grown. Food crops, such as wheat, can also be compost crops. The large amount of straw or stalk produced is food for the compost pile.

Composting also happens underground: One cereal rye plant can produce 3 miles of roots per day, and 387 miles of roots and 6,603 miles of root hairs per growing season.

Growing compost crops when we are not growing food crops helps preserve the soil's health. We can then use these plants to make compost. Compost provides not only nutrients but also organic matter, which is good for the soil in many different ways (see chapter 5). Compost crops can also add organic matter directly to the soil in the form of their roots, which are left behind after the plants have been harvested. The roots are an especially valuable form of organic matter. Gardeners have noticed a difference in the fertility of beds that have had compost crops grown in them and those that have not. Compost crops "feed" the soil.

One good compost crop combination is a mixture of wheat, cereal rye, fava beans, and vetch. The extensive roots of the wheat and rye will enrich the soil. The fava beans and grains act as supports for the vetch, which sews them all together in a kind of living fabric that is less likely to fall over in wind, rain, or snow. Fava beans and vetch also add nitrogen to the soil if they are harvested when about 10 percent to 50 percent of their flowers are in bloom. The straw from the wheat and cereal rye provides carbon for the compost pile.

Specific instructions for growing compost crops will be discussed in chapter 8.

CALORIE CROPS: Beginning to Grow a Complete Diet in Your Garden

If we really want to grow our own food, we will need to plant crops that are high in calories, such as dry beans, flour, corn, potatoes, and grains.

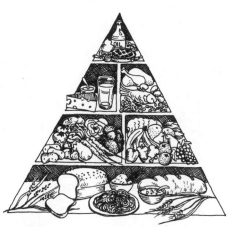

The U.S. Department of Agriculture[1] now states that we should eat two to four times more grain/cereal and dry bean crops than vegetable crops. These foods, along with fruits and nuts, are ones we can grow abundantly with Biointensive practices right in our own backyards. It is possible to grow all our food needs easily in a small area if we are eating a vegetarian diet, and as much as 77 percent of our food needs if we include meat in our diet.

A diet that is nutritionally sound needs to include an adequate amount of calories: the most important nutritional element and the most challenging one to grow in a small area. If we eat enough calories in a varied diet, we are almost certain to be getting enough protein.

When thinking about gardening, we must consider how to grow crops that will provide as many calories as possible in a given area. Dry beans can provide a lot of calories per pound, but it takes a lot of space to grow enough dry beans to provide all or most of our calories. Grains are also efficient producers of calories per pound.

We can get a lot more potatoes out of a given area than dry beans. Even though a pound of potatoes has less than one-fifth the calories that are in a pound of dry pinto beans, a small patch of potatoes produces a lot more calories in a given area than an equal area of pinto beans.

[1] USDA Food Pyramid from *EarthSave* 3, nos. 2-3, Spring and Summer 1992: p. 22.

The graph below helps you compare how many calories you get per pound from each of the calorie crops listed. From this graph, you can see that beans and wheat contain many more calories per pound than potatoes, so it looks as though beans and wheat would be much better calorie crops than potatoes.

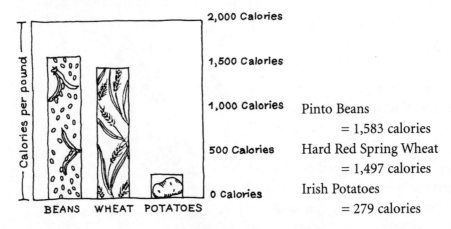

Pinto Beans
    = 1,583 calories
Hard Red Spring Wheat
    = 1,497 calories
Irish Potatoes
    = 279 calories

However, we need to look at what happens in the garden. The graph below shows how much space you will need[2] to grow one pound of each of these crops.

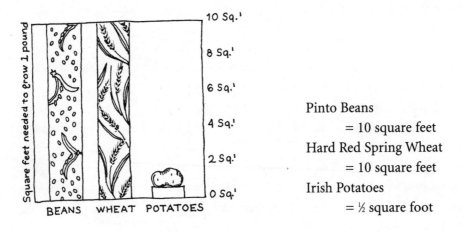

Pinto Beans
    = 10 square feet
Hard Red Spring Wheat
    = 10 square feet
Irish Potatoes
    = ½ square foot

You can see that it takes a very small area to grow one pound of potatoes and a much greater area to grow one pound of beans or wheat. This is because potatoes produce a much higher yield per unit of area than beans and wheat. The Biointensive midrange yield for potatoes is 200 pounds per 100 square feet, while the Biointensive midrange yield for beans and wheat is 10 pounds per 100 square feet.

[2] Based on a midrange yield.

The following graph shows how many square feet are needed to grow one person's calorie requirements for one year, assuming an average of 2,400 calories per day, which comes to 876,000 calories per year.

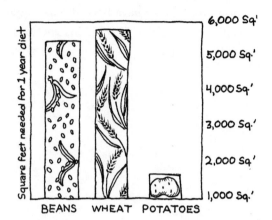

Pinto Beans
        = 5,475 square feet
Hard Red Spring Wheat
        = 5,840 square feet
Irish Potatoes
        = 1,570 square feet

So you can see that although potatoes do not have nearly as many calories per pound as wheat or beans, potatoes are a more efficient calorie crop than beans or wheat in the garden.

Other crops that can be very calorie-efficient, like potatoes, are sweet potatoes, garlic, and parsnips.

Grains like wheat, rye, barley, oats, flour corn, and amaranth take a larger area to produce a significant amount of calories, but they have an important benefit: As well as providing the gardener with calories, they provide a high amount of valuable dry material for the compost pile—which is food for the soil.

Although dry beans are a less efficient calorie crop than potatoes and do not produce much material for the compost pile, their high calorie content and the fact that they can be easily stored qualify them for a small area in our garden.

Other possible effective calorie crops are onions, turnips, and leeks. In some climates with a longer growing season and good soil, it may be possible to plant these crops twice during the growing season and obtain higher than midrange yields, in which case they may be more comparable to potatoes in efficiency.

In order to use a small amount of space in the most efficient way to produce both food for the gardener and food for the soil, a self-reliant gardener could work towards the goal of using 90 percent of the food-raising area for such calorie and carbon crops as we have been discussing and the remaining 10 percent to grow tasty fresh vegetables. Specific instructions for growing calorie crops will be discussed in chapter 9.

Chapter 2 Before You Start

The first step in turning your backyard into a productive, sustainable garden is to think about the beds: their placement, size, and arrangement.

SUN AND SHADE

Food and compost crops grow best with as much sun as possible. Eleven hours of full sunlight is best, but many plants will grow well with seven hours. Some plants, like lettuce, can manage with as few as four hours of full sunlight, but the best location for garden beds is in the full sun. Remember that the winter sun does not reach as many corners of the garden as the summer sun, and winter compost crops need all the sun they can get.

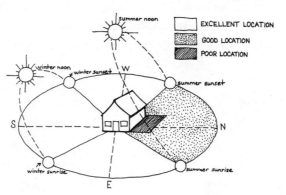

SIZE AND SHAPE OF BEDS

The size and shape of the beds in your garden will depend to some extent on the size of your backyard. The beds can be circles, ovals, squares, triangles, rectangles, or irregular shapes, but there are a few points to keep in mind.

A bed should be at least 3 feet by 3 feet for food production. This size allows the plants to establish a significant miniclimate just above the soil and allows a significant area for the roots and microorganisms below the soil surface to develop. Good conditions in both of these areas will encourage the healthy growth of the plants.

Since you should not walk on the bed after it has been prepared (unless you use a digging board to distribute your weight so that the soil will not become recompacted), you will need to be able to reach all parts of the bed easily from the path. The width of the bed should allow you to reach the middle of the bed from each side; up to 5 feet is manageable for most people. The bed can be as long as you want it to be, but you will need to walk around it to get to the other side, so about 20 to 25 feet is probably long enough.

PATHS

If you want your garden to be as productive as possible, you should not waste space on wide paths. The best width for paths is 1 foot. Narrow paths not only make the best use of the garden space, but they also encourage a healthy overall miniclimate in the garden, helping the beds to conserve more water and allowing a "humidity bubble" to cover the beds. Some people prefer wider paths for ease in walking and using a wheelbarrow, however.

GARDEN LAYOUT

Laying out several beds in a square garden arrangement, rather than in a rectangle, helps to conserve moisture and maintain a thriving ecosystem. Beds in a long, narrow arrangement dry out much more quickly than those in a wider one.

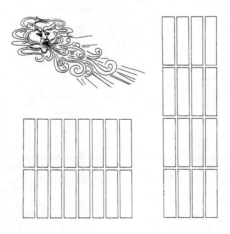

When you have decided how to arrange your beds, use stakes and string to make sure that the beds and paths are aligned properly. Once you have created a layout, continue to use that plan. As you dig and fertilize your beds year after year, your soil will continue to improve as nutrients and organic matter levels are replenished and maintained. Changing the location of beds and paths from year to year would slow down this process.

Some gardeners like to use retaining boards for their beds, but boards are not necessary. They do make a garden look tidy, but they add to the cost of setting up the garden, deplete forests, and may encourage unwelcome insects.

TOOLS

The proper tools will make gardening easier and more productive. Following are the most important tools for the garden:

For double-digging:
• a bow rake
• buckets
• a D-handled spade
• a D-handled fork
• a digging board

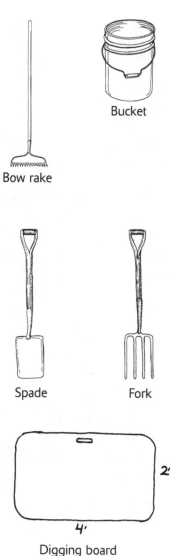

Bucket

Bow rake

D-handled spade and fork: D-handled tools are easier to dig with. When properly used, they enable you to center your energy and exert the most leverage with the least amount of effort. However, long-handled tools without a D-handle may be better for you if your back is not strong.

Spade   Fork

Digging board: You can easily make a digging board yourself. It consists of a ⅝- to ⅞-inch-thick piece of exterior plywood, 2 to 3 feet wide and 3 to 5 feet long. A 4-foot by 8-foot piece of plywood can be cut into four pieces. You can round the corners, cut out a handle hole to make carrying easier, and season it with linseed oil.

2'

4'

Digging board

For seed propagation:
• a hand fork
• a transplanting trowel
• a widger/kitchen knife/popsicle stick
• labels and a wax pencil or marker
• 1-inch chicken wire screen
• flats

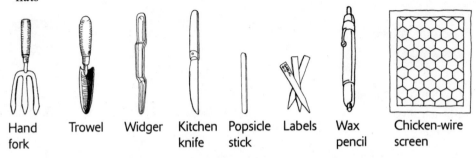

| Hand fork | Trowel | Widger | Kitchen knife | Popsicle stick | Labels | Wax pencil | Chicken-wire screen |

Flats: If you want to build your own flats, the standard flat size is 3 inches deep by 14 inches wide by 23 inches long. We also find it helpful to have some "half flats," which are 3 by 14 by 11½ inches. They can be used for smaller numbers of seedlings and are often good choices because they are lighter. If plants must remain in a flat more than 4 to 6 weeks, they will need one that is 6 inches deep, 14 inches wide, and 11⅕ inches long. (For more information on flats, see chapter 6.)

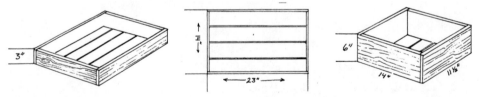

For watering:
• a Haws watering can
• a watering fan with an on/off valve (so water pressure can be changed without going back to the water spigot)
• hoses

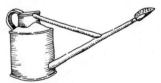

Haws watering can

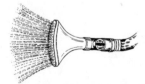

Watering fan, on/off valve, and hose

For harvesting:
• small clippers
• sheep shears (especially for grains)
• pruning shears

Small clippers   Sheep shears   Pruning shears

For information on where to buy these tools, see appendix 1.

Chapter 3 What Do You Want to Eat? Choosing What to Grow

In the next few chapters, we will describe the process of growing your first Biointensive bed. We have suggested a selection of crops for this first bed based on vegetables that Americans like to consume fresh and that they enjoy growing in their gardens. We have also suggested a growing area for each crop that can yield as much as two-thirds of the average amount consumed by one person in the United States in one year. These crops and suggested growing areas are listed in table 3.1 (see page 18). Growing instructions will be discussed in chapter 7. For now, we would just like to introduce you to the crops and techniques we recommend. As you become more experienced, you may want to add other crops and experiment with the growing areas for each.

For each crop suggested for your first Biointensive bed, table 3.1 compares Biointensive yields to the national average obtained with conventional agricultural methods. Column A shows how much of each vegetable is consumed fresh per person in the United States each year. Column B shows how much is produced by commercial U.S. agriculture per 100 square feet of soil. As you will see in column C, a 100-square-foot Biointensive bed (depending on the skill level of the gardener) can easily double or triple the crop yields for the same soil area. Eventually, as your skill and soil improve, yields may be as much as 10 or even 20 times greater than the U.S. averages.

As we discussed in chapter 1, calorie crops should be a major part of your diet and, with calorie-producing carbon crops, should eventually account for 90 percent of the growing area in your garden, with the remaining 10 percent for vegetable crops. If the crops in your garden are balanced in this way, the garden may eventually provide all of the calories, vitamins, minerals, and other nutrients that you need. To introduce you to calorie crops, we have included potatoes and onions in your first Biointensive bed, and we suggest an additional bed, perhaps in your second year, for wheat and hull-less oats during the cool weather and dry beans during the warm weather (see chapter 9).

Table 3.1

	A U.S. AVERAGE CONSUMPTION PER PERSON lbs./yr., fresh	B U.S. AVERAGE YIELD lbs./100 sq.ft.	C POSSIBLE BIOINTENSIVE YIELDS Beginning/Good/Excellent lbs./100 sq. ft.	D AREA FOR AVERAGE CONSUMPTION (sq. ft.)	E SUGGESTED INITIAL GARDEN AREA (sq. ft.)
VEGETABLE / SALAD / DESSERT CROPS					
TOMATOES	17.2	30.7	100-194-418	17.2	10
LETTUCE, LEAF	23.2	48.6	135-202-540	17.2	10
ONIONS, GREEN	D (4)	D	100-200-540	4.0	2
CORN, SWEET	7.1	15.3	17-34-68 SHELLED, WET	41.7	20
WATERMELON	13.6	24.3	50-100-320	27.2	10
CUCUMBERS	4.0	20.6	158-316-581	2.5	2
SNAP BEANS	1.5	8.2	30-72-108	5.0	2
CARROTS	7.8	58.9	100-150-1,080	7.8	4
CANTALOUPE	7.6	20	50-72-145	15.2	10
CALORIE CROPS					
POTATOES	52.0	52.6	100-200-780	52.0	25
ONIONS	17.9	68.6	100-200-540	17.9	5
				TOTAL	**100**
WHEAT (FOR CEREAL)	3.1	3.7	SEED: 4-10-26	77.5	25
OATS, HULL-LESS	3.3	D	SEED: 3-7-13+	110	25
DRY BEANS	6.0	2.7	4-10-24	150	50
				TOTAL	**100**

D — Data not available. For Green Onions, we assume an annual average consumption of 4 pounds.

Column A — Data from USDA *Agricultural Statistics,* 1987, 1978, and 1972 (except green onions).

Column B — Data from USDA *Agricultural Statistics,* 1972, and other reference sources.

Column C — Estimates based on our experience and research. Use the lowest figure if you are a beginning gardener, the middle figure if you are a good one, and the third figure if you are an excellent one.

Column D — Column A / Column C (Beginning Biointensive Yield) x 100 = approximate area needed for a beginning Biointensive gardener to grow the amount given in Column A.

Column E — Based on getting approximately ⅓ to ⅔ of the average U.S. consumption with beginning Biointensive yields and only one crop in a 4-month growing season. You can also get similar results in a 3-month growing season by using short-season varieties. If you have a 6-month growing season, you may be able to grow more than one crop. See "Crops per Growing Season" that follows.

YOUR GROWING SEASON

Your growing season will be a major factor in determining what crops to grow and when to grow them. The length of your growing season is determined by when frosts occur in your area. Experienced gardeners plan their garden activities around the first soft frost and the first hard frost in the autumn, and the last hard frost and the last soft frost in the spring. The time between the last soft frost in the spring and the first soft frost in the autumn is considered to be the optimal growing season for a particular area. In some areas, the rain determines the growing season. See "My Garden Climate" on page 20.

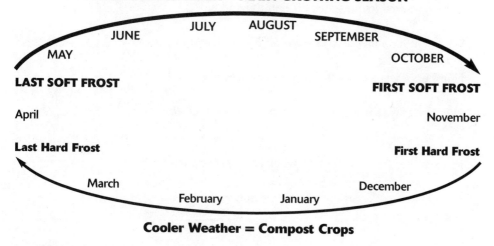

Soft frost: In a soft frost, the temperature drops a few degrees below freezing (32°F) for a short time. This may affect more delicate plants.
Hard frost: A hard frost is colder than a soft frost, for a longer period. This may kill many plants that are not frost-hardy.

Knowing the length of your growing season is important as you choose seed varieties to grow and as you plan your garden activities.

If you have a 3-month growing season, plan carefully and select seed varieties that will mature in the shortest possible time. Pay particular attention to potato, onion, and dry bean varieties in order to get the highest calorie crop yields out of your short growing season.

A 4-month growing season is a better length for a successful garden. You can choose from a greater number of later-maturing varieties and expect higher yields with this longer season.

MY GARDEN CLIMATE

Seasonal information:

First SOFT Frost Date:_____   First HARD Frost Date:_____

Last HARD Frost Date:_____   Last SOFT Frost Date:_____

Date nighttime low reaches 60°F in the spring: _____

Date nighttime low drops below 60°F in the autumn: _____

Number of weeks/months of temperatures over 95°F: _____

Number of weeks/months of temperatures under 28°F: _____

Main Spring Planting Date (1 week after last soft frost):   _____

Main Growing Period (from spring planting date
until first soft frost):   _____ to _____

You can check with your neighbors or your local agricultural extension agent about the climatic conditions for your area.

If you have a 5- or 6-month growing season, use the warmest 3 to 4 months for growing your vegetables, for the best results. If your growing season is longer than 6 months, choose the warmest 6 months of that period as you plan your gardening adventure. You can check with your local agricultural extension agent to learn how to extend your growing season.[1] Experienced neighbors are good sources of advice as well.

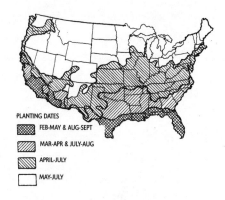

PLANTING DATES

FEB-MAY & AUG-SEPT

MAR-APR & JULY-AUG

APRIL-JULY

MAY-JULY

It is also important to be aware of your growing season because it may affect how many crops you grow per season. If your climate is favorable, you will be able to grow more than one crop per season of certain vegetables. The table below indicates the maximum number of crops that may be possible in various growing areas:

CROPS PER GROWING SEASON

	(LENGTH OF GROWING SEASON)		
	3 MO.	4 MO.	6+ MO.
Lettuce	1	2	3
Green Onions	1	2	3
Corn	1	1	2
Cucumbers	1	1	2
Carrots	1	2	2

CHOOSING SEED VARIETIES

For people whose food comes from the supermarket, a watermelon is just a watermelon, and a tomato is a (frequently tasteless) tomato. But the backyard gardener who begins to explore the seed catalogs will quickly discover that watermelons can grow in individual-serving sizes and in a variety of colors and can even have wonderful differences in flavor. As for tomatoes, you can choose a Rutgers, a Fireball, a Lincoln, a Mars, and so many others. Choosing a seed variety should take into account:

[1] *The Backyard Homestead* (pp. 158-161) also contains information on extending your growing season.

- Your growing season. For a short growing season, choose an early variety.
- Your taste preferences. Yellow, white, or red sweet corn, for example.
- Plant characteristics. Bush or pole beans, for instance.
- Amount of daylight. Some onions, for example, are adapted to areas with shorter days, others to areas with longer days.

It is well worth shopping among several seed catalogs when choosing your varieties. You may find different strains of the same variety that mature earlier or later than others. How quickly a crop matures depends on the climate, and the maturity time (or in-ground time) indicated in seed catalogs assumes optimal growing conditions in a climate that is good for the crop involved. In your particular garden climate, a variety may mature earlier than, later than, or in the same number of days as the catalog indicates.

With vegetable seeds widely available in supermarkets and hardware stores, it is easy to take seeds for granted. Yet 92 percent of all crop varieties in agriculture may be nonexistent by the year 2000, at the current rate of loss of genetic diversity. One of the best ways to preserve plant diversity is by growing and saving your own seed (see chapter 12).

In order to grow and save your own seed, you must start with open-pollinated seed, that is, seed produced from flowers pollinated naturally and easily by wind, bees, and other wild insects. The seed companies recommended below offer open-pollinated seed.

- Seed Savers Exchange (SSE) (3076 North Winn Road, Decorah, IA 52101) is doing valuable work in the area of preserving a wide variety of open-pollinated seeds. Their *Garden Seed Inventory,* 5th ed., contains a wealth of information about more vegetables than you can probably name. Members can exchange seeds.

- Bountiful Gardens, a project of Ecology Action, has put together a collection of seeds, to make your work easier at the beginning (see appendix 1). A Bountiful Gardens seed packet contains enough seeds to sow one 100-square-foot bed, unless otherwise noted, making planning easier.

It would be impossible to include every excellent seed company in this book. (A good seed company to support sells only seed with a high germination rate, which produces healthy plants with good vigor, and it specializes in, or at least emphasizes, open-pollinated varieties.) The ones we suggest here are to help you in your initial choice of open-pollinated varieties. For addresses of seed companies recommended below, see appendix 1.

When you are ready to start choosing your own varieties, here are some possibilities to explore:

Tomatoes: Choose a 3-month variety. The Bountiful Gardens choice is Rutgers (74 days). Garden City Seeds has many open-pollinated, northern-acclimated varieties.

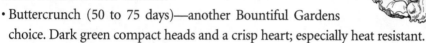

Leaf lettuce: The Bountiful Gardens choice and our personal favorite is the Bronze Arrow variety (60 days). It handles heat well, has a good flavor, and grows well spring through autumn. Other recommended varieties:
- Buttercrunch (50 to 75 days)—another Bountiful Gardens choice. Dark green compact heads and a crisp heart; especially heat resistant.
- Simpson (55 days)—Peaceful Valley Farm Supply. Starts early and tolerates heat well.

Green onions: Stokes Seeds has a good selection of 60-day varieties (be sure to specify "untreated" seed).
- Ishikura (66 days)—our personal favorite—Stokes Seeds, Peters Seed & Research. Easy to grow, matures fully in 60 days.
- White Lisbon (60 days)—Bountiful Gardens choice. Vigorous, prolific, and quick growing when grown as a green onion.
- Long White Summer (60 days)—Stokes Seeds.
- Southport White Globe (green bunching strain) (65 days)—Stokes Seeds.
- Hardy White Bunching (70 days)—Stokes Seeds.

Corn: Most seed catalogs do not carry a big selection of open-pollinated varieties, but SSE's *Garden Seed Inventory* indicates a wide choice of varieties available from many sources.
- Golden Bantam (70 to 83 days)—Bountiful Gardens choice. An old-time favorite with vigorous high-yielding plants and excellent flavor when cooked and eaten immediately after harvest.
- Montana Bantam (65 days)—Fisher's Garden Store. An extra-early strain of Golden Bantam with delicious flavor.

• Double Standard (73 days)—Johnny's Selected Seeds. A bicolored (yellow and white) corn. If you want only white corn, plant only white seeds.

Watermelon: You can choose from five different colors: red, pink, yellow, white, or orange.
• New Hampshire Midget (65 to 82 days)—Vermont Bean Seed. A personal-sized watermelon, at four to six pounds.
• Sugar Baby (68 to 86 days)—Bountiful Gardens choice. A little larger, at six to twelve pounds. Very productive and hardy; will ripen in areas where other varieties do not produce.

Cucumbers: A bush variety, rather than a vining one, is easier to grow in a small garden.
• Straight Nine (66 days)—Bountiful Gardens choice. Prolific and vigorous, it will remain green in heat and drought.
• Marketmore 86 (63 to 68 days)—Stokes Seeds (specify "untreated" seed). Sweet fruits with no bitterness under the skin; small vine or semi-bush growth habit; disease-resistant.
• Straight Eight (52 to 75 days)—Abundant Life Seed Foundation. Early, prolific, and vigorous.
• Lemon (65 days)—Peaceful Valley Farm Supply. Looks like a lemon, but you can eat it like an apple.

Bush snap beans: Bush beans bear sooner than pole beans and require no trellising.
• Derby (57 days)—a Bountiful Gardens choice. Strong upright plants with long thin pods.
• Blue Lake Oregon Bush (60 days)—Nichols Garden Nursery. Vigorous plants and beans with excellent flavor.
• Bountiful (42 to 51 days)—Vermont Bean Seed, R. H. Shumway's. Broad flat pods.
• Baffin (60 days)—a Bountiful Gardens choice. Produces pencil-slim short beans without strings.
• Kentucky Wonder Bush (65 days)—Vermont Bean Seed, R. H. Shumway's. Round fleshy pods with red seeds.

- Royalty Purple Pod (65 days)—J. L. Hudson. Purple bushes with purple flowers and purple beans that turn green when cooked.
- Roc D'Or (57 days)—Shepherd's Garden Seeds. A wax (yellow) snap bean with slender pods and a delicate buttery flavor.

Carrots: Burpee's catalog has a diagram showing the shapes and lengths of different carrot varieties.

- Danvers varieties (65 to 75 days)—widely available.
- Nantes varieties (62 to 70 days)—widely available.
- Nantes Tip Top (60 to 70 days)—Bountiful Gardens choice. Very early, good in heavy soils, and easy to pull.

Cantaloupe: The two varieties listed below are smooth-skinned and therefore less prone to rotting before harvest, but they are *not* short-season melons (not advised for cooler climates). Both are available from Bountiful Gardens.

- Haogen (90 to 95 days)—a green melon. Pale-yellow skin and medium-green flesh tinged with salmon around the seed cavity; vigorous vines produce heavy crops.
- Vedrantais (92 days)—striped skin and vivid orange flesh; ripens even in cool areas; wonderful flavor.

Potatoes: Choose from over 70 varieties, many of them organically grown, described in the Ronniger's catalog. Select a 90-day (or less) variety for a 3-month growing season. The varieties below are some of those listed by Ronniger's as early-maturing (65 days or more).

- Anoka—white. Earliest of the white varieties, stores well.
- Yukon Gold—yellow. Extra early; excellent yields; stores well.
- Warba—pink. Golden skin splashed with reddish pink and lighter pink eyes; ugly but delicious, long storing, and very early.
- Red Norland—red. Earliest of the red varieties; heavy yields and great taste.
- Caribe—blue. Lavender skin and white flesh; often grows very large.

Onions: The onions you grow may be either "keepers" that store well or "eaters" that do not. The two varieties below are keepers.

• Southport White Globe (65 to 120 days)—Bountiful Gardens choice. Best white keeper.
• New York Early (98 days)—Stokes Seeds (be sure to specify "untreated" seed). Yellow onion with hard bulb.

Wheat: The only sources for a variety of small quantities of grain seeds (enough for 100 to 1,000 square feet per package) are Bountiful Gardens and Johnny's Selected Seeds. Hard Red Spring Wheat is the Bountiful Gardens choice.

Hull-less oats: Regular oats are harder to clean. If you grow hull-less oats, you can thresh and clean the seeds without special equipment. Available from Bountiful Gardens or KUSA.

Dry beans: Available from Vermont Bean Seed or Johnny's Selected Seeds. You can choose among Pinto, Black, Red or White Kidney, and "Tri-Color." Pinto beans have slightly more calories per pound than other dry beans. In short-season areas, you can use the following 85- or 90-day varieties from Vermont Bean Seed Company:

• Red Peanut bean
• French Horticultural bean
• Great Northern White bean
• Swedish Brown bean
• Jacob's Cattle bean

• Pinto bean
• Pink bean
• Red Mexican bean
• Yellow Eye bean
• Black Turtle Soup bean

A short-season variety from Bountiful Gardens is the Taylor's Dwarf Horticultural bean, which can be used as a snap bean when young, as a green shell bean at 60 days, or as a dry bean at 80 days.

Chapter 4   Preparing a Biointensive Bed: Double-Digging

The key to a productive, healthy garden is the preparation of the growing beds. A well-prepared bed with loose soil to a depth of 24 inches allows the roots of the plants to grow evenly and to provide a steady supply of nutrients to the rest of the plant. Water is able to move through the soil freely, and weeds are easy to pull out. The plant roots have so much loose soil to grow into that more plants can grow in a given area, and this means more food from a smaller garden.

The goal of double-digging is to produce a "living sponge cake" in the soil, to a depth of 24 inches, with 50 percent pore space for air and water—optimally half of the pore space for each. (The other 50 percent of the soil is mineral matter, including rock fragments, and a small amount of organic matter.) In a new garden, the sponge cake  may turn out to be only 15 or 18 inches deep, but the microorganisms, the worms, the plant roots, and water will usually cause it to become a little deeper each year.

Any soil starts with soil particles—sand, silt, and clay in varying proportions—which constitute its texture. The roots (both living and dead) of the plants and the "sticky threads" produced by the soil microorganisms "sew" these particles together to provide a loosened aerated structure—the "living sponge cake" mentioned above. Once a good structure has been established by double-digging, it may be better to use surface culti-vation, the loosening of the upper two inches of the soil with a cultivating tool, for several years. In this way, the developed structure and soil organic matter are better preserved. Whenever the lower soil becomes compacted, the bed may be double-dug again to encourage the reestablishment of a well-aerated structure.

The best time to double-dig is in the spring, just when seedlings are ready to be transplanted into the bed. Seedlings grow best in newly loosened soil. If you are starting a new bed, it is also possible to single-dig (to loosen the soil 12 inches deep with a fork) in the fall and sow compost crops (see chapter 8). Then, in the spring, the double-digging will be that much easier.

STARTING A NEW BED

Before starting a new bed, put in stakes to mark each corner and connect the stakes with string. Depending on the condition of your soil, you may also need to do one or more of the following things in the order indicated:

1. If the soil is dry and hard, water it well (for as much as two hours with a sprinkler, if necessary) and let the water seep in for two days.

2. Loosen the soil 12 inches deep with a spading fork.

3. Remove any grass and weeds, including their roots. These[1] can go into the compost pile.

4. Water lightly for a day or two (five minutes or so per 100 square feet), or even longer if the clods are particularly large.

5. Let the soil rest for one day.

DOUBLE-DIGGING

Stand on a digging board (see chapter 2) so that your weight is distributed evenly and does not recompact the soil.

1. Across the narrow end of the bed, dig a trench 1 foot wide and 1 foot deep with a spade. Put the soil into buckets or a wheelbarrow, or pile it on the ground. The soil can then be put in a bin to use for making compost and flat soil, or it can go back into the bed to fill the last trench after the double-digging is completed.

---

[1] With the exception of crabgrass and bermuda grass, which should be thoroughly sun-dried for several months to completely kill them before they are added to the compost pile.

The last trench will not really need this soil because of the increased volume of the aerated soil in the bed, while soil used in making compost will be returned to the bed as part of the cured compost to be added to the bed later.

2. Loosen the soil in this trench an additional 12 inches with a spading fork. Dig the fork in to its full depth (or as deep as possible) and push the handle downward so the fork tines lever through the soil, loosening and aerating it. If the fork will not go through easily, pull it out a little and then push down. You should go only as deep as the tool will loosen easily. The next time you double-dig that bed, you will be able to go a little deeper.

If the soil in the lower trench is dry, water the loosened soil well before continuing. It is easier to get water down into the lower 12 inches of soil at this point than it is after the bed preparation has been completed.

If you are planting potatoes, it is easiest to plant them while you are double-digging. See the explanation on page 69.

3. Dig out the upper part of the second trench, 1 foot deep and 1 foot wide, with the spade. Dig the spade in to its full depth (or as deep as possible), lift the soil out on the spade pan, tip the spade pan downwards, and slide the loosened, aerated soil into the upper part of the first trench. Try to mix the soil layers as little as possible. Different microorganisms live in different soil layers—the less their living quarters are disturbed when the bed is dug, the more ready they will be to get on with their business of providing nutrients to the newly planted seedlings. Move each spadeful of soil forward in the same way until you have dug across the entire trench.

4. Loosen the lower 12 inches of soil in the second trench with the fork.

5. Continue in this way with the third trench and as many more trenches as you need to finish the bed.

Step 7:
Shaping

6. After the third or fourth trench (and every three to four trenches after that), rake the accumulated soil forward and level the double-dug portion of the bed. There will be less soil to move around when you reach the end of the bed and have less energy to move it. (You will not need the soil from the first trench to fill in the last trench, if you are using that soil for compost and flat mix.)

Step 8:
Spreading

7. When you have loosened the lower part of the last trench, rake the whole bed level. (Add the soil from the first trench, if you are not using it for other purposes.)

8. Spread a ½- to 1-inch layer of cured compost over the surface of the bed.

9. Sift the cured compost into the top 2 to 4 inches of the bed with a spading fork.

Step 9:
Sifting

Put compost on your bed and plant your seedlings as soon as possible after double-digging. If you cannot transplant your seedlings immediately, cover the double-dug bed with a shade net and keep the soil evenly moist to keep the microorganisms alive. Put the compost on the bed just before transplanting.

AVOIDING RECOMPACTION

Once the bed has been dug, try not to walk on it. One of the reasons for double-digging is to put air into the soil. Walking on the bed will recompact the soil. When planting the seedlings in the bed, using a digging board will allow you to distribute your weight over a wider area and minimize compaction.

Compaction destroys the structure of the soil. You have very little control over the texture of your soil—it is either sandy or clayey or something in between—but there are several things you can do to improve the structure of your soil, how your soil holds together. One solution is aerating the soil by double-digging. Another is adding organic matter to the soil in the form of compost (see chapter 5).

BY HAND?

Some people prefer to let a machine do their digging for them, but your garden soil will not benefit from rototilling. A rototiller destroys the earthworms and other soil creatures that help make your soil fertile. It also compacts the subsoil and destroys the soil's structure. Dr. Robert Parnes, author of *Fertile Soil*, notes that if we are to be sensitive to soil processes, we should avoid rototillers.[2]

HOW LONG SHOULD IT TAKE?

An expert can double-dig an established bed in one to two hours, but the first time you double-dig, it may take you all day to prepare a 100-square-foot bed, especially if the soil has never been double-dug before. As you become more familiar with what double-digging is all about, and as your garden gets more used to being double-dug, it will gradually take less and less time and effort to dig a bed.

The important thing is to take your time and learn to do it well. Increased speed will come from experience and skill—not from rushing, which will only tire you out.

USING YOUR BODY

When double-digging is properly done, your whole body weight does most of the work, with a little help from your knees and arms. If you feel excessive pressure on your back, you should stop and think about how to put less pressure on it. Use your body weight to push the spade and the fork into the soil.

[2] Robert Parnes, *Fertile Soil: A Grower's Guide to Organic & Inorganic Fertilizers* (Ag Access, 1990), p. 6.

Be sure to place your foot on the spade or the fork so that it is under your arch just in front of your heel. Your body weight is used more efficiently that way. Lift the spade only as high as you need to and let the soil slide off on its own as you tip the spade. When loosening the soil in the lower trench, use your body weight, rather than your leg and arm muscles, to push the fork through the soil.

If double-digging really seems like it will be too much for you, try to have a friend or neighbor do it for you. You might also consider single-digging and using much wider spacing for the plants.

A BIOINTENSIVE DOUBLE-DUG BED = A LAZY BED

When some people hear the term double-digging, they groan: "It's too hard." "It takes too much time." "It's too much work." "It isn't worth it." When other people hear double-digging, they smile. They think of it as exercise, rather than work. They know that a double-dug bed really is a lazy bed, because they can get a good yield in a much smaller area with less digging overall. They like the fact that double-digging keeps them in touch with the soil in their garden. They know lazy beds are fun!

Chapter 5 What to Feed a Biointensive Bed: Compost

For people who are used to depending on the supermarket for food, it is easy to forget that what we eat depends entirely on fertile soil. Sir Albert Howard, a pioneer of the organic agriculture movement, considered that the fertility of the soil determines the future of civilization.[1] The North African desert, for example, used to be the grain-growing area for Rome, until the soil was strip-mined of nutrients by improper farming practices.

Nature manages the fertility of the soil quite effectively with the natural cycles of life and death, growth and decay. As animals and plants live and grow, the animals' residues and the plants' leaves and roots enrich the soil of their environment. When the animals and plants die, moist soil helps microorganisms decompose the remains and transform them into organic matter and nutrients that replenish the soil and promote new life and growth. Nature is expert at recycling all wastes, so organic materials, major minerals, and trace minerals are continually being returned to the soil to nourish new growth.

THE BENEFITS OF COMPOST

Healthy plants in our gardens need a steady supply of nutrients. They can get 96 percent of these nutrients from air, water, and the sun (through the process of photosynthesis). If they cannot get the remaining 4 percent, however, they will not

[1] Sir Albert Howard, *An Agricultural Testament* (New York: Oxford University Press, 1943, out of print), p. 20.

grow well or provide us with healthy food. Compost, mixed into the soil, can supply these important nutrients if the compost materials have them. Compost improves the structure of the soil, making it easier to work, increasing its ability to hold water and air, and reducing the likelihood of erosion. Seeds grow into seedlings more rapidly in composted soil.

Compost is much better for the soil than chemical fertilizers, which do not add organic matter and some of which can leach out of the soil if the plants do not use them immediately. A compost pile also recycles garden debris, leaves, and kitchen waste into food for the soil.

THE DECOMPOSITION PROCESS

The decomposition process that goes on in the compost pile is carried out by a succession of microscopic organisms, including bacteria and fungi, and larger organisms, such as earthworms. Providing the ideal conditions for these organisms is what makes a good compost pile. The compost pile needs:

Air. Beneficial bacteria need air to breathe, so compost materials should be piled up loosely, but not too loosely; too much air is not good, either.

Moisture. Soil organisms need enough water to keep them alive, but not too much. You do not want to drown them. The pile should be wet, but not too wet, like a well-wrung-out sponge.

A variety of materials. The greater the variety of materials in a pile, the greater the variety of microbial life, and therefore the higher the quality of the compost and soil. In addition, greater microbial diversity reduces the likelihood of plant diseases.

Warmth. Microorganisms are most active during the warmer months of the year, when the rate of decomposition is greater, but it is important to build compost any time you have materials, even when the weather is cooler and decomposition is slower.

As the decomposition process begins, the activity of the microorganisms will cause the pile to heat up. Some microorganisms will die and others will take over, continuing the process. Eventually, the soil organisms will change the original organic materials into a more stable form of organic matter called *humus*. Humus is a living fertilizer, alive with microorganisms consuming other microorganisms that have broken down, recombined, and transformed the original organic matter. The nutrients in the humus are easily available to the plants in a slow, natural, continual process. What wonderful gardens there will be when we all develop a better sense of humus!

MATERIALS FOR A COMPOST PILE
The compost pile needs three kinds of materials:

Dry vegetation. Dry grass and weeds, leaves, straw, hay, and dry compost crops, including some woodier materials, such as broken-up corn stalks, provide organic carbon that is the energy source for all life forms.

Green vegetation. Fresh weeds, green grass, kitchen wastes, including a small amount of bones (but no meat—you do not need dogs and raccoons digging through your compost pile—or large amounts of oil), and green compost crops provide nitrogen that enables the microorganisms to develop their bodies, which are necessary to digest their carbon energy source.

Do Not Put in
the Compost Pile
• cat and dog
  manure
• diseased plants
• poisonous
  plants

Soil. Good bed soil with valuable microorganisms will help to start the decomposition process. The soil will keep down flies and odors, help the pile to hold water, and therefore allow the pile to decompose more slowly, which will ensure an easier-to-maintain compost pile.

Some people like to keep their compost under control in a bin, and a few people use a drum or an enclosure of some kind. This is not necessary, but if you prefer to use some sort of container, make sure the compost has enough air to breathe, so the correct kind of decomposition can take place.

BUILDING A COMPOST PILE
When building your pile, think about the layers that make up a dinner casserole—like a lasagna.

1. First, with a spading fork, loosen the soil 12 inches deep where you will build your pile. This area should be at least 3 feet square (4 feet or 5 feet would be even better if you have enough space and material), so the pile will have enough mass to ensure good decomposition. Loosening the soil helps to provide good drainage and aeration. Remember to leave enough space to turn the partially decomposed pile (see 7 below).

2. Put down a 3-inch layer of rough materials, which can help to aerate the pile: twigs, small branches, corn or sunflower stalks, caneberry or rosebush prunings, and so on.

3. Make your compost "lasagna" layers, watering each layer as you go:
- a 2-inch layer of dry materials
- a 2-inch layer of green materials
- a layer of soil which lightly covers the materials, or about half of a 5-gallon bucket for a 3-foot-by-3-foot compost pile

Step 4

4. Continue to add layers until your pile is about 3 feet high. If your pile is bigger at the base, you can pile the materials 4 feet high or more (but watch that the top of the pile does not start to slide). You can use a pitchfork to pull out the sides of the pile as you add layers, to keep the pile square.

5. Cover the top of the pile with extra soil, to maintain the moisture in the pile. A light layer of straw on top of the soil during the rainy season will keep out excess moisture and will prevent the pile from becoming soggy.

Step 5

6. Water the pile as needed to keep it moist. Check the moisture in the middle of the pile from time to time; it is easy to either underwater or overwater the pile.

Step 7

Turned pile ◄——— Original Pile

7. Turn the pile after about three to six weeks. The purpose of turning is to bring the drier, less-decomposed material on the outside to the inside and the more decomposed material to the outside. A good tool to use is a pitchfork, since it is lighter than a spading fork and is shaped to allow easy turning of the material. Start by loosening the soil in an area about one-half to two-thirds the original area (since the pile has shrunk) and add a layer of rough materials at the bottom. Move the materials from the original pile to the new pile, bringing the drier materials to the inside. Add water as you go, if necessary, to be sure that the turned pile is evenly moist.

8. Let the pile decompose, or "cook," for a total of three to six months. The compost is ready to use when
  • most of the original ingredients are unrecognizable,
  • its smell is fresh and woodsy like fresh spring water, and
  • the material is dark brown or black, soft and crumbly.

9. If you are not ready to use the compost when it is cured, spread it out and let it dry. It is important not to let the pile decompose too long, or the materials will turn into topsoil rather than compost and will lose the high-quality organic matter that has been so carefully built up.

This recipe may make building compost sound more complicated than it is. The important thing is just to go ahead and build your compost pile as the materials become available, without worrying too much about the details at the beginning. We recommend this low-maintenance approach, since it is easy and produces such a good result.

The three most important elements in building compost are to
  • have enough air in the pile,
  • use as many different compost materials as you can, and
  • keep the compost moist enough.

As you learn to better understand the composting process and as your garden produces more and more material for you to use, you will be able to improve your technique.

Compost Pile

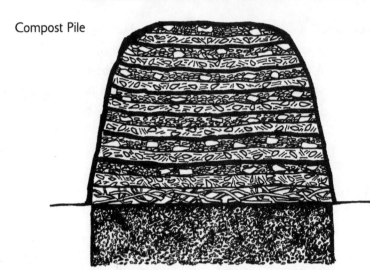

USING YOUR COMPOST

The best time to put compost in your growing beds is in the spring, just before transplanting the seedlings for the major growing season. As a general rule, you can spread ½ to 1 inch of cured compost over the surface of the bed. This comes to approximately six to twelve 5-gallon buckets per 100-square-foot bed. Then work the compost evenly into the top 2 to 4 inches of the soil, using a sifting motion with a spading fork (see chapter 4). Generally, one application of compost per 4-month growing season is adequate.

Chapter 6 Seedlings

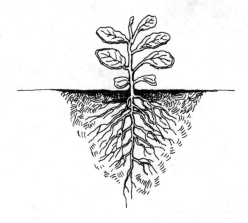

Now that your Biointensive bed has been prepared and the compost has been spread, you have a choice as to whether to sow seeds directly into the bed or to use seedlings.

Transplanting seedlings involves more advance planning and more time, but in a small garden, it has several advantages:

1. Transplanted seedlings make better use of bed space. Seeds can take from 5 days to 12 weeks or more to reach seedling size. If that growing is done in a flat, something else can be growing in the bed in the meantime.

2. You can be reasonably sure that each transplanted seedling will grow into a healthy mature plant. Not all seeds germinate, so no matter how carefully you sow seeds directly in the bed, you can end up with gaps between plants and, therefore, bare soil that allows evaporation.

3. Plants grow better if they are evenly spaced. Some seeds are sown by broadcasting, scattering them over the soil. Broadcast seeds—no matter how evenly you try to scatter them—will inevitably fall in a random pattern, with some closer and some farther apart than the optimal spacing for best plant growth. Plants that are

too close together compete with each other for light, water, and nutrients. When plants are too far apart, the soil around them may become compacted, more water may evaporate, and space is wasted.

The roots of evenly spaced transplanted seedlings can find nutrients and grow more easily, and the leaves of the plants will cover and protect the soil, creating a good miniclimate, so there is better protection for the soil. Carbon dioxide is captured under the leaf canopy of closely spaced plants, where the plants need it for optimal growth.

4. Transplanting stimulates growth. When you transplant a seedling into a double-dug, composted bed that is fluffy, aerated, and full of nutrients, you give it a second "meal" of nutrients, air, and moisture after its first "meal" in the flat. Also, if the seeds are sown directly in the bed, while the seeds are germinating and growing into seedlings, the soil will begin to recompact after its initial digging. Because of this, the soil will not be as loose for the plants to grow in once the seedling stage is reached.

5. It takes a lot less water for seedlings in a flat (½ gallon per day) than for seedlings in a bed (10 to 20 or more gallons per day).

FLATS AND FLAT SOIL

To raise seedlings, you will need flats and flat soil. Flats should be 3 inches deep to encourage good root growth after germination. The standard 3-inch-deep flat (for use with the master charts in chapter 7) is 14 inches wide by 23 inches long. A flat this size full of soil and moisture weighs about 40 pounds. A bigger flat will be very heavy and awkward to carry. A half-size flat, 14 inches by 11½ inches, is much easier to carry and especially handy for smaller gardens.

Six-inch-deep flats are good for seedlings that need to stay in the flat more than 4 to 6 weeks, to develop deeper roots, such as peppers, tomatoes, and members of the cabbage family. Six-inch-deep flats should be 14 inches by 11½ inches, the half-flat size, for lighter weight and easier handling.

A good simple flat soil mix is one part sifted compost and one part bed soil (saved from the first trench when you double-dig). "Old" flat soil that has been used to raise seedlings can be stored in a bin. Although some of the nutrients will have been depleted, the soil will still be rich in nutrients and organic matter, so it can be used to make new flat mix. In this case, the recipe is one part old flat soil, one part sifted compost, and one part bed soil. As your bed soil and your compost improve, your flat soil and seedlings will also improve.

SOWING SEEDS

When you are ready to sow your seeds in the flat, fill the flat with moist (but not too wet) flat soil, making the soil level with the top of the sides and making sure the corners are filled in.

Broadcasting

Some seeds are sown by broadcasting, that is, scattering them evenly over the soil surface.

Others, especially larger seeds, are placed on the soil 1 or 2 inches apart. A piece of 1-inch-mesh chicken wire is helpful for keeping the seeds well spaced. Put a seed in every hole for 1-inch centers, or in every other hole (using a hexagonal pattern, see p. 45) for 2-inch centers. Cover the seeds with a layer of flat soil that is as deep as the seed is high when it is resting on top of the soil, pat the seeds and flat soil down lightly for beter seed-to-soil contact, and water well.

Sowing on centers using a chicken-wire screen

FLAT SEEDING TYPES

Some seedlings can go straight from the flat to the bed. Others that need a longer time in the flat to develop their root systems will need to be "pricked out" into a second (and sometimes a third) flat. The following table will help you make a right choice.

CROP	SOW SEED IN 3-INCH DEEP FLAT	PRICK OUT 3-INCH DEEP FLAT	PRICK OUT 6-INCH DEEP FLAT
BEANS	1-INCH CENTERS		
CARROTS	BROADCAST		
CORN	1-INCH CENTERS		
CUCUMBERS	2-INCH CENTERS		
LETTUCE	BROADCAST	1.5-INCH CENTERS	
MELONS	2-INCH CENTERS		
OATS	1-INCH CENTERS		
ONIONS	BROADCAST		
POTATOES	SEE P. 69		
RYE	1-INCH CENTERS		
TOMATOES	1-INCH CENTERS		2-INCH CENTERS
WATERMELON	2-INCH CENTERS		
WHEAT	1-INCH CENTERS		

We have recommended in this book that carrots be sown directly in the bed, and many gardeners would also sow beans and corn directly in the bed. However, we have had much better results when we transplant these crops—although some skill is needed in transplanting to obtain well-shaped carrots.

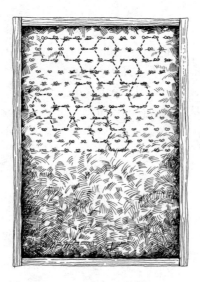

PRICKING OUT

Seedlings from broadcast seed are ready to be pricked out after their cotyledons (the first "seed leaves" that appear, although they are not the true leaves) have appeared and before the roots are too long to handle easily. The second pricking out should be done, if necessary, when the leaves of the seedlings have just begun to touch each other.

1. To prick out seedlings, fill a 3-inch- or 6-inch-deep flat with flat soil and mound the soil slightly (remember to fill in the corners).

2. Use a widger (see chapter 2) or kitchen knife to loosen the soil under the seedlings growing in the flat so that you can lift out one seedling at a time, holding it by its cotyledons and keeping as much soil on the roots as possible.

Step 3

3. Then put the widger or kitchen knife into the soil of the second flat at a slight backward angle, just behind where the seedling should be.

Step 4

4. Pull the widger toward you to open up a hole.

5. Drop the roots of the seedling into the hole, letting it go a little deeper than it was when it was growing in the first flat.

Step 5

6. Lift the widger out, and let the soil fall around the seedling. If the soil does not fall evenly around the seedling, gently fill in any holes around the seedling with the widger. It is not necessary to spend time carefully pushing the soil up around the seedling; when you water the flat, the soil will settle in around the stem and roots. The seedlings should be arranged on offset, or hexagonal, centers (see page 45) to maximize the space in the flat and to optimize the miniclimate that will develop around the seedlings as they grow.

Step 6

(See chapter 7 for how to figure out how many flats you need to plant and prick out.)

TRANSPLANTING

Generally, seedlings are ready to be transplanted into the bed when their leaves are well developed and their roots are forking and vigorous. For most seedlings, root growth should be equal to or greater than leaf growth. Some seedlings, though, will develop roots much faster than leaves. Fava beans ready for transplanting, for example, need to have only a slight amount of green visible—at that point, the root may already be 2 to 3 or more inches long.

Step 1

The best time of day to transplant is in the early evening. The cooler air makes it easier for seedlings to get established in their new environment.

Water your seedlings every three or four rows if you are planting a large area, and remember to keep the soil in the seedling flat moist.

Step 2a

As when pricking out, handle the seedlings gently, holding them by the leaves rather than the roots. If you have enough seedlings to choose from, choose the most vigorous and well-developed seedlings to transplant. Use a hand fork to loosen the soil in the flat so that you can lift each seedling out with as much soil as possible.

Step 2b

1. Open up a hole with a trowel, using the trowel in the same way as the widger (see page 43).

2. Drop the seedling in, to a depth up to its first true leaves (you can bury the cotyledons). Keep the soil loose (though not too loose); the watering will settle the soil around the roots.

Step 3

3. You may put your digging board on the bed to stand and sit on while you are transplanting. Move the board back as needed, loosening with a hand fork the soil that was just compacted by the digging board.

If you have any seedlings left over, save them until you are sure that all the ones you have transplanted will survive. If necessary, after a week or two, you can replace any seedlings that have not survived in the bed.

HEXAGONAL SPACING

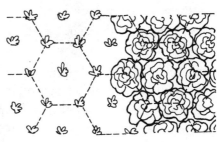

The best way to plant your flats or beds is to use offset, or hexagonal, spacing. You can get about 10 percent more plants in a bed if they are planted on hexagonal centers rather than in rows. Each plant variety needs a certain optimal amount of space for its best growth. If plants are arranged on square spacing, there will be unoccupied space that will allow some soil compaction from watering and increased evaporation.

18 plants on offset spacing

With offset, or hexagonal, spacing, the leaves of the plants reach out and touch each other on all sides, thus establishing a miniclimate that enhances the plants' growth. This miniclimate is also known as a "living mulch." The Greeks believed, and biologists know, that there is the most life where the four elements—earth, air, fire/heat/sun, and water—come together. Thus, the most important part of the plant universe is the area about 2 inches above and 2 inches below the ground around the plant. If plant leaves can protect all of the soil in a bed, the growing conditions for the plants will be more stable, and both leaves and roots will benefit.

16 plants on square spacing in same area

WATERING

The newly transplanted seedlings in your bed need to have adequate moisture. The best way to water is to create as light a "rain" as possible and to focus on watering the soil, rather than the plants. A Haws watering can, which sprays the water up into the air, and a watering fan with an on/off valve attached to a hose will do the best watering. Water falling on the bed gently will compact the soil less and will not damage the seedlings.

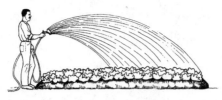

The best time of day to water is in the late afternoon. The garden may also benefit from a midday watering if needed and when that is possible. (In humid climates, be sure to allow enough time after watering for the water to evaporate off of the leaves before the air cools.) How often and how much you water depends on your weather and your soil.

You will gradually learn how much water your particular soil needs at various times of the year. After watering in the evening, check the soil the following morning. Poke your finger into the soil in different parts of the bed. If the soil is evenly moist for the first 2 inches and continues to be moist below this level, you are giving the bed enough water. If the soil is dry or soggy, you need more or less water. The edges of a bed dry out more quickly than the middle, due to more exposure to the sun, air, and wind, so give the edges two to three times more water than the middle of the bed.

Minigreenhouse with the doors flipped open

MINIGREENHOUSES

A minigreenhouse made from plastic sheeting and wood[1] can increase the temperature of the soil and the air surrounding the plants and allow the gardener to get an early start on the growing season and to extend the growing season in the autumn. The double-walled construction of the design can keep the inside temperature above the freezing point when the outside temperature falls as low as 20°F. This makes the unit a good season-extender for crops.

[1] For plans and instructions, see *The Backyard Homestead, Mini-Farm and Garden Log Book* (Willits, CA: Ecology Action, 1993).

Chapter 7   Planning and Planting Crops

PLANNING

Taking the time to put together a garden plan during the winter months when you are not busy outside will save you a lot of time and make it easy to coordinate the various activities involved in starting your garden in the spring.

For planning, you will need:
- the master chart in this chapter (or the master charts in *How to Grow More Vegetables*, 5th ed., pages 80–107),
- a current calendar,
- a list of the crops you want to grow,
- a calculator, and
- a garden plan.

Use columnar-ruled paper to create a garden plan, or make a photocopy of the blank garden plan provided on page 50–51. To create your own, identify the following columns across the top of the paper:
- Crop and Variety
- Sq Ft
- Centers
- Maximum No. of Plants per 100 sq ft
- Maximum No. of Plants for Actual Area

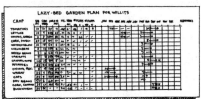

• No. of Seeds Needed for Actual Area
• Ounces Seed for Actual Area
• No. of Flats to Sow and Centers
• No. of Flats to Prick Out and Centers
• A column for each month
• Remarks

The "Crops" column and the "Remarks" column need to be wider than the others; the "Crops" column should be big enough for the full name of the crop, and the "Remarks" column can be used for notes, names of seed companies, and so on.

The following pages contain two garden plans. One is blank and can be photo-copied for your own use. The other is a sample plan for an Ecology Action Biointensive bed in Willits, California. Refer to this sample plan to help you under-stand the garden planning instructions that follow. The plans use the following abbreviations:

BC = Broadcast   TP = Transplant (into the bed)
F = Flat (sow seeds in the flat)   H = Harvest
PO = Prick out (into a second flat)

THE MASTER CHART

In chapter 3 we provide a list of twelve crops we feel would be a good place to start for a first 100-square-foot Biointensive garden. The crops chosen represent our suggested combination of vegetable/salad/dessert crops and calorie crops such as potatoes and onions. Three more calorie crops (wheat, oats, and beans) are also listed as good choices for a second 100-square-foot bed of calorie crops. In this chapter we provide a master chart (see pages 54-55), which contains all the information you need to plan your Biointensive garden with the crops we have chosen. This chart is based on the master charts in *How to Grow More Vegetables*, 5th ed., pages 80-107. This master chart also provides planning information for several recommended compost crops, which will be discussed in more detail in chapter 8, along with the second bed of calo-rie crops, which is discussed in chapter 9. For now, we will focus on the information in the master chart needed to plan your first bed, based on the crops and planting areas recommended in chapter 3. The figures in the master chart are given for a 100-square-foot area and will need to be adjusted for the area you intend to plant. Although we will later explain how to adjust the figures in the master chart for any desired planting area, start by filling in column one on your garden plan with the square feet recommended for each crop in column E in table 3.1 (page 18). Since all of the amounts in the master chart are based on a 100-square-foot bed, you can use the planting area for each crop as a percentage of that size of bed. Since table 3.1 recommends an initial planting area of 20 square feet of tomatoes, for example, that is 20 percent of the 100 square feet, and you will multiply the figures in the master chart by .20 (that is, $^{20}\!/_{100}$).

USING THE MASTER CHART

As you can see, some of the information in the master chart can be directly transferred to your garden plan. Use column CC in the master chart, for example, to fill in the in-bed spacing information in column 2 on your garden plan. Do the same for column 3 of the garden plan, using column DD in the master chart. Find, too, the corresponding master chart information for columns 8 (the first number in FF) and 10 (the second number in FF). To fill in the remaining columns in your garden plan, you will need to adjust the master chart figures for your planting areas.

FIGURING OUT HOW MUCH TO PLANT

A simple equation will allow you to figure out how much to grow in your own garden. For example, if you are growing a 100-square-foot bed of corn, you would look in column DD and find that you will need 84 plants. If you want to grow only 20 square feet of corn, however (as recommended in table 3.1), you will multiply 84 by $^{20}\!/_{100}$ or .20. You will need a maximum of 16.8 (or 17) corn seedlings to transplant, a figure you can record in column 4 of your garden plan.

Although you will ultimately transplant only 17 plants to the bed, you will need to sow more than 17 seeds in the flat, because they may not all germinate.

To determine how many seeds to sow in the flat, divide 17 by the germination rate for corn in column AA of the master chart ($17 \div 0.75 = 22.67$). This figure indicates that you will need to sow 23 seeds to be sure you will have 17 seedlings ready to transplant. Record this figure in column 5 of your garden plan. To figure the actual ounces of seed (column 6 in the garden plan) simply multiply the ounces of seed per 100 square feet (column BB) by the percentage of that area you will actually plant (in this case 20 square feet, or 20 percent). Therefore, 1.1 ounces of corn (column BB) times .20 (20 percent) is .22 ounces of corn seed.

GARDEN PLAN

		1	2	3	4	5	6	7	8	9	10
Crop -Variety		Sq. Ft.	Cen- ters	Maximum Number of Plants		Amount of Seed Needed for Actual Area		Number of Flats To Sow		Number of Flats To P.O.	
				/100	Actual	No.	Ounces	No.	Centers	No.	Centers

Jan.	Feb.	Mar.	Apr.	May	Jun.	Jul.	Aug.	Sep.	Oct.	Nov.	Dec.

BC = Broadcast   F = Flat   H = Harvest   PO = Prick out   TP = Transplant

SAMPLE BIOINTESIVE BED GARDEN PLAN FOR WILLITS

	1	2	3	4	5	6	7	8	9	10
Crop -Variety	Sq. Ft.	Cen- ters	Maximum Number of Plants		Amount of Seed Needed for Actual Area		Number of Flats To Sow		Number of Flats To P.O.	
			/100	Actual	No.	Ounces	No.	Centers	No.	Centers
Tomatoes -Rutgers	10	21	35	4	6 seeds	.0004	.02	1	.06	2
Lettuce -Bronze Arrow	10	9	248	25	32 seeds	.0012	0.1	BC	.23	1.5
Onions, Green -Ishikura	2	3	2,507	50	72 seeds	.0078	.28	BC	-	-
Corn, Sweet -Montana Bantam	20	15	84	17	23 seeds	.22	.09	1	-	-
Watermelon -Sugar baby	10	18	53	5	7 seeds	.034	.11	2	-	-
Cucumbers -Marketmore 86	2	12	159	2	3 seeds	.004	.05	2	-	-
Snap Beans, Bush -Roc Dior	2	6	621	12	16 seeds	.16	.06	1	-	-
Carrots -Nantes TipTop	4	3	2,507	100	182 seeds	.008	-	-	-	-
Cantaloupe -Cantalun	10	15	84	8	11 seeds	.009	.17	2	-	-
Potatoes -Red Norland	25	9"C, 9"deep	248	62	-	5.8- 7.75 lbs	-	-	-	-
Onions, Regular -New York Early	5	4	1,343	67	96 seeds	.01	.38	BC	-	-
Wheat -Hard Red Spring	25	5	833	208	297 seeds	.6	1.18	1	-	-
Oats -Hull-less	25	5	833	208	297 seeds	.31	1.18	1	-	-
Dry Beans -Black Turtle	50	6	621	310	442 seeds	6.35	1.76	1	-	-
Corn for Compost -Montana Bantam	25	12	159	40	53 seeds	.52	.21	1	-	-
Buckwheat	25	BC	-	-	-	.65	-	-	-	-

Jan.	Feb.	Mar.	Apr.	May	Jun.	Jul.	Aug.	Sep.	Oct.	Nov.	Dec.
	2/21 →		4/1 F								
		3/21 →		5/1 PO 5/21 TP			8/15 H →				
			4/14 →	5/1 F							
			4/21 →	5/7 PO 5/21 TP		7/21 H →					
		3/21 →	4/7 F	5/21 TP		7/21 H →					
				5/16-18 F 5/21 TP							
			4/21-28F	5/21 TP		7/26 H →					
			4/21-28F	5/21 TP		7/21 H →			10/4 BC compost crops		
				5/7-14 F 5/21 TP		7/21 H →					
				5/21 BC		7/21 H →					
			4/21-28F	5/21 TP			8/21 H →				
		Order	4/21 sprout	5/21 TP		7/26 H					
1/7-21F				5/21 TP			8/30 H				
1/15-21 F	2/1 TP					7/15 H					
1/15-21 F	2/1 TP					7/15 H					
				5/7-14F 5/21 TP			8/21 H		10/4 BC compost crops		
						7/10-12 F 7/15 TP		9/30 H			
						7/15 BC		9/30 H			

BC = Broadcast   F = Flat   H = Harvest   PO = Prick out   TP = Transplant

PLANNING YOUR GARDEN—

	AA GERMINATION RATE	BB OUNCES SEED /100 sq. ft.	CC IN-BED SPACING	DD MAX. PLANTS /100 sq. ft.	EE FLAT or BC
VEGETABLE / SALAD / DESSERT CROPS					
TOMATOES	.75	.004	21	35	F
LETTUCE, LEAF	.80	.012	9	248	F
ONIONS, GREEN	.70	.39	3	2,507	F
CORN, SWEET	.75	1.1	15	84	F
WATERMELON	.70	.34	18	53	F
CUCUMBERS	.80	.2	12	159	F
SNAP BEANS	.75	8.3	6	621	F
CARROTS	.55	.2	3	2,507	BC
CANTALOUPE	.75	.09	15	84	F
CALORIE CROPS					
POTATOES	-	23.25-31 LBS.	9"C, 9"D	248	-
ONIONS, REGULAR	.70	.21	4	1,343	F
WHEAT (FOR CEREAL)	.70	2.4	5	833	F
OATS, HULL-LESS	.70	1.25	5	833	F
DRY BEANS	.70	12.7	6	621	F
SUMMER COMPOST CROPS					
CORN, SWEET	.75	2.1	12	159	F
BUCKWHEAT	.70	2.6	BROADCAST	-	BC
WINTER COMPOST CROPS					
WHEAT (COMPOST)	.70	2.4 (2.0 INTERPL.)	5	833 (694 INTERPL.)	F
CEREAL RYE	.70	2.4 (.4 INTERPL.)	5	833 (138 INTERPL.)	F
FAVA BEANS	.70	18.5 (1 INTERPL.)	21	35	F
VETCH	.70	5.5 (.62 INTERPL.)	BROADCAST	-	BC

—MASTER CHART

FF IN-FLAT SPACING	GG PLANTS /FLAT	HH WEEKS IN FLAT	II WEEKS TO MATURITY	JJ WEEKS HARVEST	
					VEGETABLE / SALAD / DESSERT CROPS
1 / 2	187 / 60	4-8 / 3-4	8-13	17+	TOMATOES
BC / 1.5	200 / 111	1-2 / 2-3	6-8	1-3	LETTUCE, LEAF
BC	175	6-8	8-17	SEE P. 62	ONIONS, GREEN
1	187	3-5 DAYS	9-13	-	CORN, SWEET
2	42	3-4	10-13	13	WATERMELON
2	48	3-4	7-10	26	CUCUMBERS
1	187	1-2	8	12	SNAP BEANS
-	-	-	9-11	4-6	CARROTS
2	45	3-4	12-17	13	CANTALOUPE
					CALORIE CROPS
	SEE TEXT FOR INSTRUCTIONS.		17	-	POTATOES
BC(1)	175	6-10	14-17	-	ONIONS, REGULAR
1	175	1-2	16-18	-	WHEAT (FOR CEREAL)
1	175	1-2	13-17	-	OATS, HULL-LESS
1	175	1-2	12	8	DRY BEANS
					SUMMER COMPOST CROPS
1	187	3-5 DAYS	9-13	-	CORN, SWEET
-	-	-	9-13	-	BUCKWHEAT
					WINTER COMPOST CROPS
1	175	1-2	16-18	-	WHEAT (COMPOST)
1	175	1-2	16-18	-	CEREAL RYE
1	175	1-2	17-26	-	FAVA BEANS
-	-	-	-	-	VETCH

Notes on Master Chart on Pages 54–55.

Column AA—Minimum germination rate that is legal for seeds available through commercial seed companies.

Column BB—Adjusted for the germination rate, offset spacing, and curved surface. May be less for corn, watermelon, and oats, depending on seed size.

Column CC—In-bed spacing in inches.

Column DD—Maximum number of plants that will fit in a 100-square-foot bed with the in-bed spacing indicated in column CC. This takes into account the curved surface of the double-dug bed and the offset spacing. This is a maximum. If your soil structure does not produce a curved surface after double-digging, fewer plants will fit in your bed.

Column EE—Sow seeds in flats (F) or broadcast seeds directly into the bed (BC).

Column FF—Left-hand number is for initial seeding in flat. Right-hand number is for later pricked-out spacing in another flat, when that is recommended. For lettuce, the pricked-out flat should be 3 inches deep. For tomatoes and most other crops that will be pricked out, the second flat should be 6 inches deep.

Column GG—See note for column FF. See chapters 2 and 6 for standard flat size. Approximately 250 seeds/plants will fit on 1-inch centers; approximately 60 will fit in a standard flat on 2-inch centers. The numbers in this column have been adjusted for the germination rate of each crop.

Column HH—See note for column FF. The range of weeks given depends on the temperature. In warmer climates, use the shorter time; in cooler climates, use the longer time. Experience will eventually be your guide.

Column II—Approximate number of weeks to maturity after transplanting.

Column JJ—Harvesting period in weeks, depending on variety and weather.

HOW MANY FLATS TO SOW

To figure out how many flats are needed (column 7 on your garden plan), look first at the number of living plants you need for your area (column 4 on your garden plan). Then look at column GG in the master chart for the number of plants that you can expect to get from a standard flat given the germination rate for that crop and the proper spacing. Because the number in column GG has already been adjusted for the germination rate (see note for column GG), simply divide the number of plants you need by the (left-hand) number in column GG. This will tell you what proportion of a standard flat you need to sow.

A similar calculation will tell you what proportion of a flat you will need for plants that are pricked out (column 9). Since we have already taken the germination rate into account, simply divide the number in column 4 by the right-hand number in column GG to find the number of flats you will need.

CUSTOMIZING YOUR BIOINTENSIVE BED

Depending on your personal gardening needs, objectives, and preferences, you may decide you want to grow more or less of the crops listed here or to incorporate crops not included here. The figures given here and in the sample garden plan for Willits on pages 52–53 are based on the type and amount of crops recommended in table 3.1 on page 18. When deciding how much to grow in your own garden, you may want to consider about how much of a particular crop you would like to eat per week. Once you know how many pounds of a crop you will use per week during harvest time, then look in column JJ in the master chart to see how many weeks that particular crop can be harvested. Multiply these two numbers to determine how many total pounds of that crop you will need that season. Then consult table 3.1 on page 18 to find the beginning Biointensive yield for that crop (in column C). This reflects the number of pounds of a particular crop a 100-square-foot planting area will yield in a season. Simply divide the desired yield by the beginning yield given in table 3.1, and multiply by 100 square feet to get the planting area required to achieve your desired yield.

You can then plug this new planting area into column 1 in your garden plan in place of the recommended area given in table 3.1. Remember that you will need to adjust the figures in columns 4, 6, 8, and 10 of your garden plan to reflect this new area. Recall that this is accomplished by dividing the new area by 100 square feet and multiplying the result by the number given in the master chart.

Here is an example of how to customize your snap bean crop to yield 2 pounds of beans per week:

- Look at column JJ in the master chart for snap beans: Snap beans can be harvested over a 12-week period. Let us assume 10 weeks for planning purposes, since the plants may not be as productive near the end as at the beginning.

- Multiply 2 pounds of beans per week by 10 weeks to get 20 pounds total. Table 3.1 (page 18), column C, shows that at beginning Biointensive yields, a 100-square-foot bed with produce 30 pounds of beans from one planting.

- Divide the desired yield (20 pounds) by the given yield (30 pounds), then multiply by 100 square feet. You will need approximately 67 square feet to grow 20 pounds of beans.

- Enter 67 square feet in column 1 of your garden plan. Remember to adjust the other garden plan calculations for this new area.

To customize your garden by adding crops not discussed in this book, refer to the master charts in *How to Grow More Vegetables*, 5th ed., pages 80–107.

THE DATE COLUMNS

If your area does not have frost, you can plant all year, with the hot-weather crops, such as tomatoes, being planted when daytime temperatures reach 80°F and nighttime temperatures are preferably 60°F or higher.

The goal of the date columns in your garden plan is to provide you with a concise gardening schedule, from the time you sow seeds in the flats until the time you harvest. The first step in developing this schedule is to establish your main spring planting date. This is generally one week after the last soft frost (see "My Garden Climate" in chapter 3). It is possible to plant cool-weather crops, such as onions, lettuce, potatoes, and carrots, earlier than that, but for the purposes of this beginning garden, we will assume that all the crops will be planted at about the same time. In Willits, we assume that we will have our last soft frost on May 15, so our main spring planting date is May 21. Record your own transplant date for each crop in your garden plan, using the plan on page 53 as an example.

Now, look at column HH to see how long the plants are in the flat before they are transplanted. Count backwards from the transplanting date to determine the date to sow your seeds in flats. While you are still learning, it is best to use the higher number of weeks the seedlings are in the flat, if there is a range. Record these dates in your garden plan for each crop.

To find out the maturity date, or the time to harvest (H), see column II, and count forward from your transplant date the number of weeks it will take the crop to mature. This will tell you when you can expect to start harvesting your crop. Record these dates in your garden plan as well.

The last dates to schedule are when to sow autumn-winter compost crops. Most compost crops should be sown or transplanted before the first rain or soft frost, about 4 to 6 weeks before your first hard frost (Willits, October 1–15; your area, _____). Compost crops will be discussed further in chapter 8.

GROWING INSTRUCTIONS

The following paragraphs describe how to use the master chart and garden plan to grow specific crops. The transplanting date is assumed to be about one week after the last soft frost in Willits (May 21). The dates need to be adjusted for your area. In fact, because seedlings often ignore the schedule made by the gardener, all dates given are approximations.

Tomatoes (10 sq. ft.):

WHEN TO START	SEED NEEDED (ACTUAL)	SOW	MAX NO. SEEDLINGS NEEDED	PRICK OUT	TRANSPLANT
• 7-12 weeks before expected planting date: • 2/21-4/1 in Willits, • _____ in your area.	• .0004 oz., • 6 seeds.	• in a 3-inch-deep flat, • on 1-inch centers, • using about 2 percent of the flat.	4	• When about 2-3 inches tall, • after about 4-8 weeks, • into a 6-inch deep flat, • on 2-inch centers	• When seedlings are about 5-6 inches tall, • on 21-inch centers, • on 5/21 in Willits, • on _____ in your area.

Growing instructions: Use .004 ounce (⅛ level teaspoon) of seed per 100 square feet (col. BB) or .0004 ounce for 10 square feet (.004 ounce x 10 sq ft ÷ 100 sq ft = .0004 ounce). On 21-inch centers (col. CC), a 100-square-foot bed will hold up to 35 plants (col. DD), so a 10-square-foot area will hold a maximum of 4 plants (35 plants x 10 sq ft ÷ 100 sq ft = 3.5 plants). To ensure 4 tomato seedlings to transplant, you will need to sow 6 tomato seeds (4 ÷ .75 germination rate [col. AA] = 5.3). The 6 seeds on 1-inch centers (col. FF left) will take up approximately ⅟₅₀ of a standard flat (4 ÷ 187 [col. GG left] = .02). Therefore, sow the seeds on 1-inch centers (col. FF left) in ⅟₅₀ of a flat (col. EE) 7 to 12 weeks (total of weeks in col. HH) before the expected planting date (Willits, February 21 to April 1) and leave the flat in a warm area. After 4 to 8 weeks (col. HH left), when the seedlings are 2 to 3 inches tall, prick them out on 2-inch centers (col. FF right) in a 6-inch-deep flat. You will need to use ⅞₁₀₀ of a full-sized flat (4 ÷ 60 [col. GG right] = .07) or ¹³⁄₁₀₀ of a flat if you use the half-sized flat. Transplant the seedlings into the bed on 21-inch centers (col. CC) when the seedlings are about 5 to 6 inches tall. Put a 7- to 8-foot stake beside each seedling (making sure at least 1 foot of the stake is in the ground), and as the plant grows, tie the branches loosely (using a figure-eight loop) to the stake. Let the plant grow as it likes; it is not necessary to pinch off any shoots.

Harvest when the tomatoes are full and ripe. Keep the ripe ones picked to encourage further fruiting.

Lettuce (10 square feet): If the temperature is over 80°F, it is important to freeze lettuce seed in a tightly closed jar for 4 days before planting it, to help trigger germination. There is no harm in keeping the jar in the freezer in between sowings during the summer.

Lettuce is a cool-weather crop, so it will appreciate being shaded by another crop, such as corn or tomatoes, or having a 30-percent shade net over it once the temperature goes higher than 70° to 85°F. Taking the shade net off after the heat of the day and putting it back on in the morning before the heat of the day will help the lettuce to grow faster. Also, lettuce likes midday watering in summer to keep it cool.

WHEN TO START	SEED NEEDED (ACTUAL)	SOW	MAX NO. SEEDLINGS NEEDED	PRICK OUT	TRANSPLANT
• 3-5 weeks before expected planting date: • 4/14 - 5/1 in Willits, • _____ in your area.	• .0012 oz., • about 1⁄32 tsp. • 32 seeds.	• Broadcast in a 3-inch-deep flat, • using about 12.5 percent of the flat.	25	• When cotyledons are just big enough to handle, • into a 3-inch deep flat, • on 1.5-inch centers, • using about 25 percent of the flat.	• When seedlings are about 2.5-3 inches tall, • on 9-inch centers, • on 5/21 in Willits, • on _____ in your area.

When broadcasting seeds into flats, such as with lettuce and onions, you can use much less flat space than indicated by the calculations given in these growing instructions. These calculations assume that you will be sowing on 1- or 2-inch centers. Since lettuce seedlings are pricked out after such a short period and since onion and green onion seedlings don't mind being a little crowded, you can usually broadcast the seeds into as little as one-half to one-quarter of the calculated flat space and achieve good results.

Growing instructions: Use .012 ounce (¼ teaspoon) of seed per 100 square feet (col. BB) or .0012 ounce (½ teaspoon) for 10 square feet (.012 ounce x 10 sq ft ÷ 100 sq ft = .0012 ounce). On 9-inch centers (col. CC), a 100-square-foot bed will hold up to 248 plants (col. DD), so a 10-square-foot area will hold a maximum of 25 plants (248 plants x 10 sq ft ÷ 100 sq ft = 24.8 plants). To ensure 25 lettuce seedlings to transplant, you will need to sow 32 lettuce seeds (25 ÷ .80 germination rate [col. AA] = 31.25). The 32 seeds broadcast in a flat will take up approximately ⅛ of the flat (25 plants ÷ 200 [col. GG left] = .125). Therefore, broadcast the seeds in ⅛ of a flat (col. EE) 3 to 5 weeks (total of col. HH) before the scheduled planting date (Willits, April 14 to May 1). When the cotyledons (seed leaves) are just big enough to handle, prick out the seedlings on 1½-inch centers (col. FF right) into a 3-inch-deep flat. You will need to use about ¼ of a 3-inch-deep flat (25 germinated seedlings ÷ 111 seedlings per flat [col. GG right] = .225). Transplant the seedlings into the bed on 9-inch centers (col. CC) when they are about 2½ to 3 inches tall and have strong, forking roots. Germination and growth will take longer in cool weather.

Harvest a mature head by cutting it off at ground level, or leave the plants in the ground and harvest only the outside leaves. Lettuce has the best flavor if harvested before sunrise.

Green onions (2 square feet):

WHEN TO START	SEED NEEDED (ACTUAL)	SOW	MAX NO. SEEDLINGS NEEDED	TRANSPLANT
• 6-8 weeks before expected planting date: • 3/21-4/7 in Willits, • _____ in your area.	• .0078 oz., • about 1/8 tsp. • 72 seeds.	• Broadcast in a 3-inch-deep flat, • using about 30 percent of the flat.	50	• When seedlings are pencil-lead thick, • on 3-inch centers, • on 5/21 in Willits, • on _____ in your area.

Growing instructions: Use .39 ounce (1 tablespoon + 1¼ teaspoon) of seed per 100 square feet (col. BB) or .0078 ounce (⅛ teaspoon) for 2 square feet (.39 ounce x 2 sq ft ÷ 100 = .0078 ounce). On 3-inch centers (col. CC), a 100-square-foot bed will hold up to 2,507 plants (col. DD), so a 2-square-foot area will hold a maximum of 50 plants (2,507 plants x 2 sq ft ÷ 100 sq ft = 50.14 plants). To ensure 50 green onion seedlings to transplant, you will need to sow 72 green onion seeds (50 ÷ .70 germination rate [col. AA] = 71.43). The 72 seeds broadcast (col. FF) in a flat will take up approximately ³⁄₁₀ of a the flat (50 ÷ 175 [col. GG] =.29). Therefore, broadcast the seeds into ³⁄₁₀ of a flat 6 to 8 weeks (col. HH) before the scheduled planting date (Willits, March 21 to April 7). (See notes about broadcasting seeds on page 61.) Transplant the seedlings into the bed on 3-inch centers (col. CC) when they are about the thickness of ordinary pencil lead. Have patience, and remember to stand and stretch while transplanting. You might consider planting part of the bed each day.

Harvest after 2 months (col. II) or when the plants are slightly thicker than your little finger. Green onions may be kept in the bed until you are ready to eat them.

Corn (20 square feet):

WHEN TO START	SEED NEEDED (ACTUAL)	SOW	MAX NO. SEEDLINGS NEEDED	TRANSPLANT
• 3-5 days before expected planting date: • 5/16-18 in Willits, • _____ in your area.	• .22 oz., • ⅔ Tbsp., • 23 seeds.	• in a 3-inch-deep flat, • on 1-inch centers, • using about 10 percent of the flat.	17	• When seedlings are about 1 inch tall, • on 15-inch centers, • on 5/21 in Willits, • on _____ in your area.

Growing instructions: Use 1.1 ounces (scant ¼ cup) of seed per 100 square feet (col. BB) or .22 ounce (⅔ tablespoon) for 20 square feet (1.1 ounces x 20 sq ft ÷ 100 = .22 ounce). On 15-inch centers (col. CC), a 100-square-foot bed will hold up to 84 plants (col. DD), so a 20-square-foot area will hold a maximum of 17 plants (84 plants x 20 sq ft ÷ 100 sq ft = 16.8 plants). To ensure 17 corn seedlings to transplant, you will need to sow 23 corn seeds (17 ÷ .75 germination rate [col. AA] = 22.6). The 23 seeds on 1-inch centers (col. FF) will take up

approximately ⅒ of a standard flat (17 ÷ 187 [col. GG] = .09). Therefore, sow the seed on 1-inch centers in ⅒ of a flat (col. EE) 3 to 5 days (col. HH) before the expected planting date (Willits, May 16-18). Transplant the seedlings into the bed on 15-inch centers (col. CC), taking care to keep the root as vertical as possible, when they are about 1 inch tall.

Harvest the corn when the juice in the seeds is halfway between clear and milky. You can check this by puncturing a few seeds with the edge of your fingernail.

Watermelon (10 square feet):

WHEN TO START	SEED NEEDED (ACTUAL)	SOW	MAX NO. SEEDLINGS NEEDED	TRANSPLANT
• 3-4 weeks before expected planting date: • 4/21-28 in Willits, • _____ in your area.	• .03 oz., • ¼ tsp., • 7 seeds.	• in a 3-inch-deep flat, • on 2-inch centers, • using about 10 percent of the flat.	5	• When seedlings have 2-3 true leaves, • on 18-inch centers, • on 5/21 in Willits, • on _____ in your area.

Growing Instructions: Use .34 ounce (1½ tablespoons) of seed per 100 square feet (col. BB) or .03 ounce (¼ teaspoon) for 10 square feet (.34 ounce x 10 sq ft ÷ 100 sq ft = .034 ounce). On 18-inch centers (col. CC), a 100-square-foot bed will hold up to 53 plants (col. DD), so a 10-square-foot area will hold a maximum of 5 plants (53 plants x 10 sq ft ÷ 100 sq ft = 5.3 plants). To ensure 5 watermelon seedlings to transplant, you will need to sow 7 watermelon seeds (5 ÷ .70 germination rate [col. AA] = 7.1). The 7 seeds on 2-inch centers (col. FF) will take up approximately ⅒ of a standard flat (5 ÷ 42 [col. GG] = .12). Therefore sow the seed on 2-inch centers (col. FF) in approximately ⅒ of a flat (col. EE) 3 to 4 weeks (col. HH) before the expected planting date (Willits, April 21 to 28). Transplant the seedlings into the bed on 18-inch centers (col. CC), setting the plants in up to the cotyledons (seed leaves), when they have 2 to 3 true leaves.

Harvest when the watermelon says "Plunk!" when you tap it with a knuckle. If it says "Plink!" or "Plank!" it is not yet mature enough.

Cucumbers (2 square feet):

WHEN TO START	SEED NEEDED (ACTUAL)	SOW	MAX NO. SEEDLINGS NEEDED	TRANSPLANT
• 3-4 weeks before expected planting date: • 4/21-28 in Willits, • _____ in your area.	• .004 oz., • 3 seeds.	• in a 3-inch-deep flat, • on 2-inch centers, • using about 4 percent of the flat.	2	• When seedlings have 2-3 true leaves, • on 12-inch centers, • on 5/21 in Willits, • on _____ in your area.

Growing Instructions: Use .2 ounce (2 teaspoons) of seed per 100 square feet (col. BB) or .004 ounce (.2 ounce x 2 sq ft ÷ 100 sq ft = .004 ounce) for 2 square feet. In fact, you will need only 2 plants for 2 square feet since the plants are on 12-inch centers (col. CC), so you should sow 3 seeds (2 ÷ .80 germination rate [col. AA] = 2.5). The 3 seeds on 2-inch centers (col. FF) will take up approximately ⅕ of a standard flat (2 ÷ 48 [col. GG] = .04).

Therefore, sow the seed on 2-inch centers (col. FF) in ⅕ of a flat (col. EE) 3 to 4 weeks (col. HH) before the expected planting date (Willits, April 21 to 28), keeping the flat in a warm area. Transplant the seedlings into the bed on 12-inch centers (col. CC), setting the plants in up to the cotyledons (seed leaves), when the seedlings have 2 to 3 true leaves.

Harvest when the fruits are swollen, smooth, and green, and before they begin to turn yellow.

Snap Beans (2 square feet):

WHEN TO START	SEED NEEDED (ACTUAL)	SOW	MAX NO. SEEDLINGS NEEDED	TRANSPLANT
• 1-2 weeks before expected planting date: • 5/7-14 in Willits, • _____ in your area.	• .16 oz., • 1 tsp., • 16 seeds.	• in a 3-inch-deep flat, • on 1-inch centers, • using about 6 percent of the flat.	12	• When seedlings have 2-3 true leaves, • on 6-inch centers, • on 5/21 in Willits, • on _____ in your area.

Growing Instructions: Use 8.3 ounces (1⅓ cups) of seed per 100 square feet (col. BB) or 0.16 ounce (1 slightly rounded teaspoon) for 2 square feet (8.3 ounces x 2 sq ft ÷ 100 sq ft = .16 ounce). On 6-inch centers (col. CC), a 100-square-foot bed will hold up to 621 plants (col. DD), so a 2-square-foot area will hold a maximum of 12 plants (621 plants x 2 sq ft ÷ 100 sq ft = 12.4 plants). To ensure 12 snap bean seedlings to transplant, you will need to sow 16 snap bean seeds (12 ÷ .75 germination rate [col. AA] = 16). The 16 seeds on 1-inch centers (col. FF) will take up approximately ³⁄₅₀ of a standard flat (12 ÷ 187 [col. GG] = .06). Therefore, sow the seeds on 1-inch centers (col. FF) in ³⁄₅₀ of a flat (col. EE) 1 to 2 weeks (col. HH) before the expected planting date (Willits, May 7 to 14). Transplant them into the bed on 6-inch centers (col. CC), setting the plants in up to the cotyledons (seed leaves), when they have 2 to 3 true leaves.

Harvest when the pods are bulging with seeds. You can increase your bean yield by picking ripe beans frequently.

Carrots (4 square feet):

WHEN TO START	SEED NEEDED (ACTUAL)	SOW
• On your planting date: • 5/21 in Willits, • _____ in your area.	• .008 oz., • ⅛ tsp., • 182 seeds.	Broadcast seed directly into bed.

Growing Instructions: Use .2 ounces of seed (3½ teaspoons) per 100 square feet (col. BB) or .008 ounce (⅛ teaspoon) for 4 square feet (.2 ounce x 4 sq ft ÷ 100 sq ft = .008 ounce). On 3-inch centers (col. CC), a 100-square-foot bed will hold up to 2,507 plants (col. DD), so a 4-square-foot area will hold a maximum of 100 plants (2,507 plants x 4 sq ft ÷ 100 sq ft = 100 plants). To ensure 100 carrot seedlings, you will need to sow 182 carrot seeds (100 ÷ .55 germination rate [col. AA] = 182.3). Broadcast the seed directly into 4 square feet of the bed (col. EE) on your planting date (Willits, May 21). Broadcasting the seed perfectly would result in 2 seeds per  center on 3-inch centers (col. CC), with, on average, only 1 seed per center germinating. Chop the seed in lightly with a rake, using an up-and-down motion. For best results, be sure to keep this area moist, or cover it with a shade net placed directly on the soil until you can see that the carrot seedlings are growing well.

Harvest after the carrots have been growing for 60, 75, or 90 days, according to the variety and your personal preference.

Cantaloupe (10 square feet):

WHEN TO START	SEED NEEDED (ACTUAL)	SOW	MAX NO. SEEDLINGS NEEDED	TRANSPLANT
• 3-4 weeks before expected planting date: • 4/21-28 in Willits, • _____ in your area.	• .009 oz., • ½ tsp., • 11 seeds.	• in a 3-inch-deep flat, • on 2-inch centers, • using about 20 percent of the flat.	8	• When seedlings have 2-3 true leaves, • on 15-inch centers, • on 5/21 in Willits, • on _____ in your area.

Growing Instructions: Use .09 ounce (½ tablespoon) of seed per 100 square feet (col. BB) or .009 ounce (½ teaspoon) for 10 square feet (.09 ounce x 10 sq ft ÷ 100 sq ft = .009 ounce). On 15-inch centers (col. CC), a 100-square-foot bed will hold up to 84 plants (col. DD), so a 10-square-foot area will hold a maximum of 8 plants (84 plants x 10 sq ft ÷ 100 sq ft = 8.4 plants). To ensure 8 cantaloupe seedlings to transplant, you will need to sow 11 cantaloupe seeds (8 ÷ .75 germination rate [col. AA] = 10.6). The 11 seeds on 2-inch centers (col. FF) will take up approximately ⅕ of a standard flat (8 ÷ 45 [col. GG] = .18). Therefore, sow the seed on 2-inch centers (col. FF) in ⅕ of a flat (col. EE) 3 to 4 weeks (col. HH) before the expected planting date (Willits, April 21 to 28). Transplant the seedlings into the bed on 15-inch centers (col. CC), setting the plants in up to the cotyledons (seed leaves), when the seedlings have 2 to 3 true leaves.

Harvest when the outer skin begins to change color and when the portion around the vine, which attaches the melon to the plant, begins to soften.

Potatoes (25 square feet):

WHEN TO START	SEED NEEDED (ACTUAL)	SPROUT	PLANT
• 1 month before expected planting date: • 4/21 in Willits, • _____ in your area.	• 6-8 lbs.	• Put to sprout in warm, lighted area. • When sprouts are still less than 3 inches long, • cut potatoes into pieces, • cover cut surfaces with ash, • and dry for 2-3 days.	• on 9-inch centers, • 9 inches deep, • while double-digging, • on 5/21 in Willits, • on _____ in your area.

Growing Instructions: Use 23¼ to 31 pounds for 100 square feet (col. BB) or 5⅘ to 7¾ pounds for 25 square feet (23¼ pounds x 25 sq ft ÷ 100 sq ft = 5 ⅘ pounds). Potatoes for planting should be ordered to arrive at least 1 month before the scheduled planting date. To sprout  potatoes, place them, 1 month before planting (Willits, April 21), in a warm, lighted area with 50 percent to 60 percent humidity. If they are at 90 percent humidity for 24 hours with the temperature at 70°F, they can get blight. Sprouts should not grow any longer than 3 inches.

There should be 2 to 3 "eyes" for each large-egg-sized potato, or, if the potato is very large, it should be cut up  into several pieces, each with 2 to 3 "eyes," and set out to dry for 2 to 3 days in a warm, dry place with indirect light. Covering the cut surface with wood ash will help to prevent harmful microorganisms from damaging the seed potato pieces.

Plant sprouted potatoes or potato pieces 9 inches deep on 9-inch centers (col. CC), in 25 square feet of your growing area, while you are double-digging that area (see below).

Our Potato-Planting Technique
Planting as you double-dig your bed is the easiest way we have found to plant potatoes. After the lower trench has been loosened, Irish potatoes may be placed on its surface on 9-inch centers using offset, or hexagonal, spacing (see page 45). The soil

from the next trench's upper level may then be moved forward onto them. Mark the location of the potatoes with stones or sticks in the outside paths before covering the potatoes with soil. This will help you locate where potatoes should be placed on the surface of each succeeding lower trench.

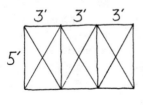

Staking Potatoes for Better Growth

Potatoes like cool weather. In many warmer areas, we have gotten higher yields by staking up the potatoes as described below. This enables the potato vines to stand up straight and create a miniclimate that keeps the plants and soil cooler.

Put 5-foot stakes (1 inch by 1 inch) 1 foot deep in the soil at the corners of the potato section and at 2½- to 3-foot intervals. Tie string to the stakes, 1 foot from the ground and at 1-foot vertical intervals, around the outside of the bed and also crisscrossing the bed, to support the plants. Be sure to water well.

Harvest any time after flowering, preferably after approximately 90 percent of the green matter has died back. Most of the potato tuber develops in the last 30 to 45 days of its growing period, so be careful not to harvest early. Use a fork to dig carefully, starting from the side of the bed. Store the potatoes in a dark, humid, cool location; if they are stored in the light, they will turn green and will not be edible.

Regular onions (5 square feet):

WHEN TO START	SEED NEEDED (ACTUAL)	SOW	MAX NO. SEEDLINGS NEEDED	TRANSPLANT
• 6-10 weeks before expected planting date: • 3/7-4/7 in Willits, • _____ in your area.	• .01 oz., • ¼ tsp., • 96 seeds.	• Broadcast in a 3-inch-deep flat, • using about 40 percent of the flat.	67	• When seedlings are pencil-lead thick, • on 4-inch centers, • on 5/21 in Willits, • on _____ in your area.

Growing instructions: Use .21 ounce (1 tablespoon) of seed per 100 square feet (col. BB) or .01 ounce (¼ teaspoon) for 5 square feet (.21 ounce x 5 sq ft ÷ 100 sq ft = .01 ounce). On 4-inch centers (col. CC), a 100-square-foot bed will hold up to 1,343 plants (col. DD), so a 5-square-foot area will hold a maximum of 67 plants (1,343 plants x 5 sq ft ÷ 100 sq ft = 67.15 plants). To ensure 67 onion seedlings to transplant, you will need to sow 96 onion seeds (67 ÷ .70 germination rate [col. AA] = 95.71). The 96 seeds broadcast in a flat (col. FF) will take up approximately ⅖ of the flat (67 plants ÷ 175 plants [col. GG] = .38). Therefore, broadcast (col. FF) the seeds into ⅖ of a flat (col. EE), 6 to 10 weeks (col. HH) before the scheduled planting date (Willits, March 7 to April 7). (See notes about broadcasting seeds on page 61.) Transplant the seedlings into the bed on 4-inch centers (col. CC) when they are about the thickness of ordinary pencil lead.

When the first onion tops begin to dry and fall over, bend down all of the tops. About 1 week later, stop watering and let the onions stay in the ground for another week or so to cure. Then, to harvest, using a digging fork or a smaller border fork, start at one end of the bed, loosen the soil under the onions and lift them out. Spread them to dry in a shady, aerated place. Leave the dry tops on, and store in a mesh bag, or braid several onion tops together to make an onion braid. If any onion stems do not dry thoroughly, eat those onions first—they will not store well.

You can cut out the root section of an onion and plant it: You will get another onion.

(See chapter 9 for growing instructions for wheat, oats, and dry beans.)

Chapter 8   Growing Compost Crops

We have been focusing on growing food for ourselves, but the only way that the soil can continue to produce food is if we also grow food for the soil, which provides sustainable soil fertility.

A fertile, healthy soil will produce healthy crops that will keep the gardener healthy, too. In order to maintain the fertility of the soil in the garden, the soil must be fed the nutrients it needs to have available for the plants, particularly if we are harvesting the vegetables and eating them without returning our wastes to the soil. Also, the soil organic matter that helps to hold nutrients and improve soil structure and water retention needs to be replenished regularly.

Growing a variety of compost crops provides a diverse mix of food for the microorganisms in the compost pile. These crops may be grown during the cooler season in many climates. If your growing season is very short and your winters are very cold, you will need to grow both a food-crop bed and a compost-crop bed during the warmest months.

	SUMMER	WINTER
Area with cold winter and short summer growing season	Food and Compost crops	—
Area with milder winter	Food Crops	Compost crops

You will need to decide how many Biointensive beds to grow, depending on your climate and your preferences.

One good mixture of compost crops is wheat, cereal rye, fava beans, and vetch. The wheat and rye develop extensive root systems that improve the soil structure, while the vetch and fava beans fix nitrogen in the nodules on their roots. The vetch twines among the taller plants and helps to support them. The straw from the mature wheat and rye plants provides carbon for the compost pile, while the vetch and fava beans, harvested green (at approximately 10 percent to 50 percent flower), provide nitrogen. If left to mature fully, the wheat and rye can also provide food for the gardener—in the optimal proportion to allow the phytase in the rye to buffer the phytates in the wheat and rye that would otherwise reduce our bodies' ability to absorb iron from the food we eat.

The compost crop seed recipe per 100 square feet:
      2 ounces (about ⅓ cup) hard red spring wheat,
      .4 ounce (about 1 tablespoon) cereal rye,
      .62 ounce (about 5¼ teaspoons) vetch, and
      1 ounce (about ¼ cup) Banner fava beans sown on 21-inch centers.

Schedule your planting date about 6 weeks before the first hard frost date (Willits, October 4).

You may single-dig your bed (loosen the soil with a spading fork). Or, if you are breaking new ground and want optimal yields, you may double-dig the bed if the soil is not too moist.

You can broadcast the wheat, rye, and vetch seeds separately and evenly over the bed, and "chop them in" lightly with a rake. The fava beans are then sown on 21-inch offset, or hexagonal, centers. Be sure the sown seeds are covered with a thin layer of soil equal to the height of the seed when it is lying flat.

Interplanted Compost Crops Sown Directly in the Bed

Broadcast wheat, rye, and vetch separately; chop in with a rake.
Sow fava beans directly on 21-inch centers.

Or, for optimal yields, you can sow the seeds in flats and transplant the seedlings into the bed.

Interplanted Compost Crops Transplanted (100 sq. ft.):

WHEN	WHAT
10-15 days before planting date (Willits: 9/19-24, your area: _____)	Sow about 50 fava bean seeds on 1-inch centers using 20 percent of a 3-inch-deep flat
5-10 days before planting date (Willits: 9/24-29, your area: _____)	Sow 2 oz. hard red spring wheat on 1-inch centers in 4 3-inch-deep flats. Sow .4 oz. cereal rye on 1-inch centers using 80 percent of a 3-inch-deep flat.
On planting date (Willits: 10/4, your area: _____)	Broadcast vetch and chop in with a rake. On 5-inch centers, transplant 5 wheat, then 1 rye, alternating. Transplant fava beans on 21-inch centers

Vetch (for 100 square feet interplanted). Use Wooly Pod or Winter Hairy vetch for very cold winter areas, Purple or Common vetch for warmer areas. When growing vetch only, use 5.5 ounces per 100 square feet. When growing vetch with other compost crops, use .62 ounces per 100 square feet. Soak the seed overnight for better germination. Broadcast the seed evenly over the bed, and "chop it in" lightly with a rake.

Fava beans (for 100 square feet interplanted). Use Banner fava beans, which can take temperatures down to 10°F. When growing fava beans only, use approximately 9.1 ounces (457 seeds) per 100 square feet if transplanted, or 6.4 ounces (320 seeds) if sown directly in the bed on 8-inch centers. When growing fava beans with other compost crops, use approximately 1 ounce (50 seeds)

75

per 100 square feet if transplanted, or .7 ounce (35 seeds) if sown directly on 21-inch centers. If you are transplanting, sow the seeds in flats on 1-inch centers, 10 to 15 days before the scheduled planting date (Willits, September 19 to 24), and transplant when the seedlings are 1 inch high and the roots are about 1 to 2 inches long. Or sow the seeds directly and cover with a thin layer of soil. (We recommend transplanting, as fava beans establish more completely when they are transplanted.) Use a digging board to distribute your weight evenly.

Wheat (for 100 square feet interplanted). Use hard red spring wheat. When growing wheat only, use 2.4 ounces per 100 square feet. When interplanting with rye, use 2 ounces per 100 square feet. Sow the seeds in flats on 1-inch centers, 5 to 10 days before the scheduled planting date (Willits, September 24 to 29). (In warmer climates or greenhouses, it can take as few as 5 days for the seed to sprout; in colder climates and outside, it can take as many as 10 days or more.) When the plants are 1 to 1½ inches tall and the roots are 1½ to 2 inches long, transplant on 5-inch centers. If interplanting wheat and rye, transplant 5 wheat plants, then 1 rye plant, and continue throughout the bed. Also, interplant the fava beans on 21-inch centers, either by transplanting or by sowing directly.

Rye (for 100 square feet interplanted). Use cereal rye (*Secale cereale*). When growing rye only, use 2.4 ounces per 100 square feet. When interplanting with wheat, use .4 ounces per 100 square feet. Sow the seeds in flats on 1-inch centers, 5 to 10 days before the scheduled planting date (Willits, September 24 to 29). Transplant after every fifth wheat plant (on 5-inch centers).

GRAZING

Compost crops will need to be cut back, or "grazed," whenever they reach 18 inches high, depending on the weather. This is done so the wind, rain, and snow will not cause them to fall over, or "lodge." They may need to be grazed two to three times during the winter. Cut them back to 6 inches above the soil, and use the material for your compost pile. Do not graze later than three months before warmer weather (Willits, February 1); the crops need the following four months to fully mature and produce seed. In Willits, we usually graze these crops about December 1 and February 1, but it varies a lot from year to year.

HARVEST

Compost crops may be ready to harvest as early as May 1 and as late as July, depending on your climate. When the fava beans and vetch are in approximately 50 percent flower, *carefully* pull out only the fava beans and vetch (the vetch will pull out easily enough; try to get the fava beans out by snapping, pulling, or cutting them, without disturbing the wheat and rye), and use this material in your compost pile. The wheat and rye should continue to mature until the plants are approximately 85 percent golden and the seed grain is crunchy, usually in June or July. A good tool for harvesting grains is a pair of sheep shears. Cut the plants as close to the ground as possible.

If seed has set (wheat sometimes does not set seed in winter), thresh the grain while the heads are still attached, or cut off the heads and clean the seed (see chapter 9). Use the straw for your compost pile; be sure to incorporate green material, such as green weeds, green grass, or even comfrey or alfalfa, along with it.

It is possible that you will have to harvest your compost crops before they are mature, in order to get your bed ready for the expected planting day (Willits, May 9). If so, cut everything off at ground level and use the material for your compost pile. Then double-dig the bed, and add compost before you transplant your seedlings.

Other possibilities for compost crops are clover, oats, barley, and agricultural mustard. Bountiful Gardens carries these compost-crop seeds and many others (see appendix 1 for address).

Chapter 9 Growing More Calories

Vegetables provide important vitamins and minerals in our diet, but many of them can be considered "green water" in terms of the energy that they provide. Our bodies also need calories for energy. This book has already introduced you to two good calorie crops: potatoes and onions. You may want to consider growing some others.

If you live in a climate (not too cold and not too hot) that will allow you to grow grains easily, you can grow these calorie crops during the cooler winter months in a second Biointensive bed. For garden fertility, you can also grow summer compost crops in the bed—corn or buckwheat, for example—during the warm months. These may also produce a significant yield of grain high in calories.

In addition to grains, dry beans are a crop with a lot of calories per pound. However, grain and bean caloric yields per unit of area are low in comparison with those of potatoes. (See the discussion in chapter 1.) Dry beans need to be grown during warm weather. In the garden space that grows dry beans during the warm summer, you can also grow interplanted compost crops, such as wheat and vetch, during the winter.

PLANNING YOUR CALORIE CROPS

The calorie crop map below shows one 100-square-foot calorie-crop bed through the year. Half of the bed will grow dry beans during the main growing season and compost crops during the cool weather. The other half will grow winter grains during the latter part of the cool weather and the beginning of the warm weather, summer compost crops during the rest of the warm weather, and interplanted winter compost crops during the first part of the cool weather. The dates given below are for the Willits climate. You will need to adjust them for your climate.

When you plant these crops for the second year, be sure to rotate the oats and wheat crops to the previous year's dry bean section, and vice versa.

Calorie-Crop Map (100 square feet)
(Progression of the growing bed through the seasons)

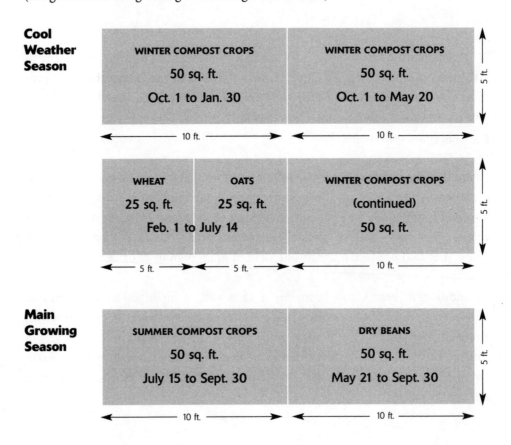

Cool Weather Season

| WINTER COMPOST CROPS 50 sq. ft. Oct. 1 to Jan. 30 | WINTER COMPOST CROPS 50 sq. ft. Oct. 1 to May 20 |
| 10 ft. | 10 ft. |

| WHEAT 25 sq. ft. Feb. 1 to July 14 | OATS 25 sq. ft. | WINTER COMPOST CROPS (continued) 50 sq. ft. |
| 5 ft. | 5 ft. | 10 ft. |

Main Growing Season

| SUMMER COMPOST CROPS 50 sq. ft. July 15 to Sept. 30 | DRY BEANS 50 sq. ft. May 21 to Sept. 30 |
| 10 ft. | 10 ft. |

Refer to the master chart in chapter 7 for details on the following crops.

We will assume that you are starting your calorie crop bed by planting winter compost crops in late September or early October, after both the dry beans and the summer compost crops have been harvested. See chapter 8 for how to grow winter compost crops.

THE GRAIN SECTION OF THE CALORIE-CROP BIOINTENSIVE BED—50 Square Feet

The wheat and oats will be transplanted on approximately February 1 in the Willits area (your area, _____).

About February 1, from 50 square feet of the bed, pull out the winter compost crops with the roots, and put this material in your compost pile. If the weather has been wet, you can cover this section of the bed with plastic 1 week before you expect to transplant the winter grains, so that it is not too wet to work with.

Wheat (25 square feet):

WHEN TO START	SEED NEEDED (ACTUAL)	SOW	MAX NO. SEEDLINGS NEEDED	TRANSPLANT
• 1-2 weeks before expected planting date: • 1/15-21 in Willits, • _____ in your area.	• .6 oz., • 1 tbsp. + 1tsp., • 297 seeds.	• in a 3-inch-deep flat, • on 1-inch centers, • using 1.2 flats.	208	• When seedlings are about 1-1.5 inches tall and roots are 1.5-2 inches long, • on 5-inch centers, • on 2/1 in Willits, • on _____ in your area.

Growing Instructions: Use 2.4 ounces (slightly rounded ⅓ cup) of hard red spring wheat per 100 square feet (col. BB) or .6 ounce (1 tablespoon + 1 teaspoon) for 25 square feet (2.4 ounces x 25 sq ft ÷ 100 sq ft = .6 ounce). On 5-inch centers (col. CC), a 100-square-foot bed will hold up to 833 plants (col. DD), so a 25-square-foot area will hold a maximum of 208 plants (833 plants x 25 sq ft ÷ 100 sq ft = 208.25 plants). To ensure 208 wheat seedlings to transplant, you will

need to sow 297 wheat seeds (208 ÷ .70 germination rate [col. AA] = 297.1). The 297 seeds on 1-inch centers (col. FF) will take up approximately 1⅙ standard flats (208 ÷ 175 [col. GG] = 1.18.) Therefore, sow the seed on 1-inch centers (col. FF) in approximately 1⅙ flats (col. EE) 1 to 2 weeks (col. HH) before the expected planting date (Willits, January 15 to 21). (In a warmer climate or a greenhouse, it can take as few as 5 days for the seed to sprout; in a colder climate and outside, it can take as many as 10 days or more.) Transplant the seedlings into the bed on 5-inch centers (col. CC) when they are about 1 to 1½ inches tall and the roots are 1½ to 2 inches long.

Harvest when the plants are dry and the seeds are crunchy when you bite one between your teeth (Willits, approximately mid-July). Cut the plants off at ground level. If you know someone who has a mechanical thresher, leave the heads on the stalks; it is easier to thresh the heads that way. If you will be threshing by hand, cut the heads off the stalks. Let them both dry thoroughly. Use the stalks with other green material for your compost pile.

Thresh the heads by spreading them out on a clean cement floor or driveway (preferably with a rough surface), putting on some clean tennis shoes (preferably with soles that are not too smooth), and doing the shuffle! When the grain has been loosened from the chaff, use two bowls or buckets and pour the grain back and forth between them outside in a stiff wind or with the air from the back end of a vacuum cleaner blowing on them, to separate the chaff from the grain. Store the grain in a clean glass jar. You can cook the wheat berries like rice for supper, or cook them a little longer for breakfast cereal.

Oats (25 square feet):

WHEN TO START	SEED NEEDED (ACTUAL)	SOW	MAX NO. SEEDLINGS NEEDED	TRANSPLANT
• 1-2 weeks before expected planting date: • 1/15-21 in Willits, • _____ in your area.	• .31 oz., • 2 tbsp., • 297 seeds.	• in a 3-inch-deep flat, • on 1-inch centers, • using 1.2 flats.	208	• When seedlings are about 1-1.5 inches tall and roots are 1.5-2 inches long, • on 5-inch centers, • on 2/1 in Willits, • on _____ in your area.

Growing Instructions: Use 1.25 ounces (⅕ cup) of hull-less oats per 100 square feet (col. BB) or 0.31 ounce (1 tablespoon) for 25 square feet (1.25 ounces x 25 sq ft ÷ 100 sq ft = 0.31 ounce). On 5-inch centers (col. CC), a 100-square-foot bed will hold up to 833 plants (col. DD), so a 25-square-foot area will hold a maximum of 208 plants (833 plants x 25 sq ft ÷ 100 sq ft = 208.25 plants). To ensure 208 oat seedlings to transplant, you will need to sow 297 oat seeds (208 ÷ .70 germination rate [col. AA] = 297.1). The 297 seeds on 1-inch centers (col. FF) will take up approximately 1⅕ standard flats (208 ÷ 175 [col. GG] = 1.18). Therefore, sow the seed on 1-inch centers (col. FF) in approximately 1⅕ flats (col. EE) 1 to 2 weeks (col. HH) before the expected planting date (Willits, January 15 to 21). (In a warmer climate or a greenhouse, it can take as few as 5 days for the seed to sprout; in a colder climate and outside, it can take as many as 10 days or more.) Transplant the seedlings into the bed on 5-inch centers (col. CC) when they are 1 to 1½ inches tall and the roots are 1½ to 2 inches long.

Harvest when the plants are dry and the seeds are crunchy when you bite one between your teeth (Willits, mid-July). Use the same harvest and threshing procedures as for wheat.

THE DRY BEAN SECTION OF THE BED

To prepare the bed, pull out the winter compost crops with the roots from the other 50 square feet of the bed and put this material in your compost pile. Double-dig this 50-square-foot area, and add compost.

Dry Beans (50 square feet):

WHEN TO START	SEED NEEDED (ACTUAL)	SOW	MAX NO. SEEDLINGS NEEDED	TRANSPLANT
• 1-2 weeks before expected planting date: • 5/7-14 in Willits, • _____ in your area.	• 6.4 oz., • 1 cup, • 442 seeds.	• in a 3-inch-deep flat, • on 1-inch centers, • using 1.75 flats.	310	• When seedlings have 2-3 true leaves, • on 6-inch centers, • on 5/21 in Willits, • on _____ in your area.

Growing Instructions: Use 12.7 ounces (2¼ cups) of seed per 100 square feet (col. BB) or 6.4 ounces (1 slightly rounded cup) for 50 square feet (12.7 ounces x 50 sq ft ÷ 100 sq ft = 6.35 ounces). On 6-inch centers (col. CC), a 100-square-foot bed will hold up to 621 plants (col. DD), so a 50-square-foot area will hold a maximum of 310 plants (621 plants x 50 sq ft ÷ 100 sq ft = 310.5 plants). To ensure 310 dry bean seedlings to transplant, you will need to sow 443 dry bean seeds (310 ÷ .70 germination rate [col. AA] = 442.8). The 442 seeds on 1-inch centers (col. FF) will take up approximately 1¾ standard flats (310 ÷ 175 [col. GG] = 1.77). Therefore, sow the seed on 1-inch centers (col. FF) in 1¾ flats (col. EE) 1 to 2 weeks (col. HH) before the expected planting date (Willits, May 7 to 14). (In a warmer climate or a greenhouse, it can take as few as 5 days for the seed to sprout; in a colder climate and outside, it can take as many as 10 days or more.) Transplant the seedlings on 6-inch centers (col. CC), setting the plants in up to the cotyledons (seed leaves), when the bean seedlings have 2 to 3 true leaves.

For maximum yields, harvest the beans at the shell-bean stage, when the beans are swollen in the pods but the pods are still green or just starting to dry, and let the beans dry; this way they will be less likely to have weevils, and the plant may produce more flowers and beans. This will allow you to have dry beans without waiting the extra month for the beans to dry on the bush. Alternatively, you may let them dry on the plant and harvest the plants when most of the beans are dry; this involves less handling but a greater possibility of weevils and a lower yield.

SUMMER COMPOST CROPS

After the grains have been harvested, double-dig that portion of the bed and plant a 60-day corn in 25 square feet and buckwheat in the other 25 square feet.

Corn for Compost (25 square feet):

Use a 60-day corn variety (for example, Montana Bantam; see chapter 3) planted on 12-inch centers. This is closer than you would plant corn for eating, so you will probably harvest only a few developed ears to eat, but the purpose of this section is to grow material for the compost pile.

WHEN TO START	SEED NEEDED (ACTUAL)	SOW	MAX NO. SEEDLINGS NEEDED	TRANSPLANT
• 3-5 days before expected planting date: • 7/10-12 in Willits, • _____ in your area.	• .52 oz., • 11.5 tbsp., • 53 seeds.	• in a 3-inch-deep flat, • on 1-inch centers, • using about 20 percent of the flat.	40	• When seedlings are about 1 inch tall, • on 2-inch centers, • on 7/15 in Willits, • on _____ in your area.

Growing Instructions: Use approximately 2.1 ounces (⅓ cup) of seed per 100 square feet (col. BB) or .52 ounce (1½ tablespoons) for 25 square feet (2.1 ounces x 25 sq ft ÷ 100 sq ft = .525 ounce). On 12-inch centers (col. CC), a 100-square-foot bed will hold up to 159 plants, so a 25-square-foot area will hold a maximum of 40 plants (159 plants x 25 sq ft ÷ 100 sq ft = 39.88 plants). To ensure 40 corn seedlings to transplant, you will need to sow 53 corn seeds (40 ÷ .75 germination rate [col. AA] = 53.33). The 53 seeds on 1-inch centers (col. FF) will take up approximately ⅕ of a standard flat (40 ÷ 187 [col. GG] = .213). Therefore, sow the seeds on 1-inch centers in ⅕ of a flat (col. EE) 3 to 5 days (col. HH) before the expected planting date (Willits, July 10 to 12). Transplant the seedlings into the bed on 12-inch centers (col. CC), taking care to keep the root as vertical as possible, when they are about 1 inch tall.

Harvest any ears when they are developed (see chapter 7), and pull the stalks out when they are as dry as possible, to use for the compost pile. In any case, you will need to get the bed ready for the winter compost crops to go in (Willits, about October 1).

Buckwheat (25 square feet): Buckwheat does not have the extensive root system that grain crops do, and it does not fix nitrogen in the soil like beans do, but it is a valuable summer compost crop. It grows quickly and protects the soil during the heat of the summer, and its flowers attract a variety of beneficial insects to your garden. Though it can be grown for buckwheat seeds, this crop is being grown as a compost crop, which also concentrates nitrogen in its body for use in the compost pile.

WHEN TO START	SEED NEEDED (ACTUAL)	SOW
• On your planting date: • 7/15 in Willits, • _____ in your area.	• .65 oz., • ¼ cup, • 16 seeds.	Broadcast seed directly into bed.

Growing instructions: Use 2.6 ounces (1 cup) of seed for 100 square feet (col. BB) or .65 ounce (¼ cup) for 25 square feet (2.6 ounces x 25 sq ft ÷ 100 sq ft = .65 ounce). Broadcast the seed evenly over the surface of the soil, then chop it in with a rake, using an up-and-down motion.

Harvest the buckwheat by cutting it off at ground level at the end of your growing season. Add the green material to the compost pile.

WINTER COMPOST CROPS

The whole bed (100 square feet) may be planted once again with winter compost crops, after both the dry beans and the summer compost crops have been harvested. See chapter 8 for how to grow the winter compost crops.

Chapter 10 Arranging What Goes into a Bed: Companion Planting

Once you have determined the area you want to grow for each crop, you can decide about the placement of the different crops in the bed. You must take into consideration not only such things as sun and shade but also which plants make good neighbors.

Map of the Bed (not to scale)

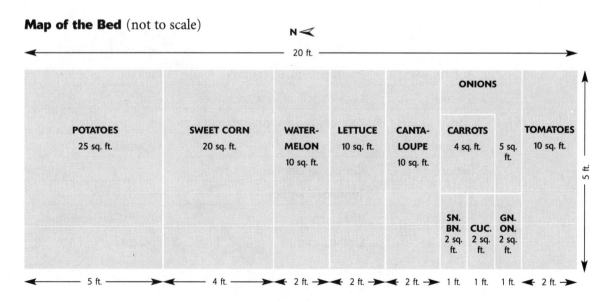

N

← 20 ft. →

| POTATOES 25 sq. ft. | SWEET CORN 20 sq. ft. | WATER-MELON 10 sq. ft. | LETTUCE 10 sq. ft. | CANTA-LOUPE 10 sq. ft. | CARROTS 4 sq. ft. | 5 sq. ft. | TOMATOES 10 sq. ft. |

ONIONS

SN. BN. 2 sq. ft. | CUC. 2 sq. ft. | GN. ON. 2 sq. ft.

5 ft.

← 5 ft. → ← 4 ft. → ← 2 ft. → ← 2 ft. → ← 2 ft. → 1 ft. 1 ft. 1 ft. ← 2 ft. →

A garden mini-ecosystem is part of a larger ecosystem, interacting with sun, shade, warmth, wind, birds, insects, and animals. Nature's ecosystem is varied and balanced, with harmonious, beneficial interrelationships. While our main focus is on growing a healthy soil, an additional goal is to make our garden reflect nature's diversity. Even weeds have a key role to play.

Companion planting involves choosing which crops to put beside each other for the best results, keeping in mind the garden as a whole.

GOOD NEIGHBORS

Although scientific documentation is scarce, gardeners have observed that some plants do better if they are grown with certain other plants. Since plant roots extend over a much wider area than can be observed with the eye, it is possible that plant roots react to each other underground, stimulating or hindering growth. Experienced gardeners have noticed that the crops proposed here for your first Biointensive bed have the following likes and dislikes when it comes to neighbors. The suggested layout of your Biointensive bed takes these into account (see page 87).

	CLOSE NEIGHBORS	DISTANT NEIGHBORS
Bush Beans	Potatoes, lettuce, tomatoes	Onions
Carrots	Leaf lettuce, onions, tomatoes	-
Corn	Potatoes, beans, cucumbers	-
Cucumbers	Beans, corn	Potatoes
Lettuce	Carrots, cucumbers	-
Onions	Tomatoes, lettuce	Beans
Potatoes	Beans, corn	Cucumbers, tomatoes
Tomatoes	Onions, carrots	Potatoes

BENEFICIAL INFLUENCES

Following are some plants that have been found by experience to be good for the garden in general. They are perennial, so they might be planted at the ends of beds, where they will not get in the way of double-digging. Some of these plants are herbs that can be enjoyed for tea or seasoning; others are weeds that we would do well to encourage in our gardens instead of trying to get rid of:

Lemon balm (tea)	Chamomile (tea)	Oregano (herb)	Marjoram (herb)
Valerian (root is medicinal)		Dandelion	Stinging nettle

CROP ROTATION

For a number of reasons, it is good not to plant the same crop in the same spot year after year. Different plants take different nutrients, and different quantities of nutrients, out of the soil. Planting the same crop in the same place in succession creates soil nutrient deficiencies and also encourages insect and disease problems.

Compost helps replenish soil nutrients, and planting different crops over time will help to maintain the nutrient balance in the soil. Planting a winter compost crop that includes grains, with their extensive root systems, and legumes (beans, vetch, clover, and so on), with their nitrogen-fixing ability, will greatly benefit the soil (see chapter 8).

SUN AND SHADE

It is easy to forget that tiny seedlings can turn into tall plants. A tall plant, such as corn, can be put where it will shade a plant that enjoys less sun, like peas, potatoes, or cucumbers. Sun-loving tomatoes can provide a cooler miniclimate for onions or parsley. Notice that the potatoes in the Biointensive bed will be shaded by the corn, and the tomatoes will shade the onions, if the bed is oriented as indicated.

Cool weather crops, like lettuce, carrots, onions, and potatoes, will do well in partial shade in warmer weather.

ATTRACTING "GOOD" BUGS

Bees and butterflies play an important part in the life cycle of plants, so a garden will benefit if it includes their favorite meals. Bees can account for up to one-third of the United States crop yield through the pollination they accomplish. Bees love blue flowers, especially borage and rosemary. Butterflies are attracted to purple, red, yellow, and orange flowers and will beautify your garden along with the flowers you plant to attract them.

Other beneficial insects are attracted to the flowers of parsley, dill, and cilantro/coriander. Try letting a few of those plants go to seed to serve as feeding stations for helpful insects.

Chapter 11 Keeping the Garden Healthy

Beginning gardeners are often inclined to worry about getting rid of insects and weeds, but it is much more enjoyable to think of insects and weeds as part of Nature's contribution to a diverse ecosystem. Weeds that compete with the plants we are trying to grow should obviously be taken out and added to the compost pile, and insects that insist on helping themselves to our garden vegetables need to be dealt with gently yet firmly. Generally, a garden will benefit from the gardener's focus on health and life rather than on death and disease.

A thriving, diverse garden with healthy soil will attract beneficial insects that will make themselves useful pollinating, cleaning up rotting debris, and eating harmful insect larvae. In fact, in a balanced mini-ecosystem, for every seven or eight good bugs, there will be only one harmful one. If we get rid of all the bad bugs in our garden, the good bugs have less to eat and have no reason to stay around to help.

Insects and disease are most likely to attack sick plants, those that are under stress for some reason. Making sure the soil has all the nutrients, soil air, soil moisture, and cured compost needed by the plants we are growing is a much better way to use our energy than looking for ways to get rid of pests. Compost made from a variety of plant materials will encourage a variety of microorganisms in the soil, and they will provide the wide range of nutrients needed for healthy plants. Careful transplanting also helps to promote uninterrupted root growth and encourages vigorous, healthy plants. The right amount of water throughout the plants' growing period will also reduce the likelihood of stress.

THE FOUR BASIC KINDS OF INSECTS	HOW TO CONTROL THEM EASILY
Chewing or biting, soft-bodied Chewing or biting, hard-bodied	Aromatic and distasteful sprays, such as garlic, onion, and pepper spray
Sucking, soft-bodied	Soap solution sprays (not detergents)
Sucking, hard-bodied	Hand picking

Garlic/Onion Tea Insect Repellent

Mash 10 cloves of garlic or a medium onion. Mix with 2 quarts/liters of water. Let it sit. Strain. Spray without diluting. (Good against nematodes.)

"The Bomb" Insecticide

Melt ½ bar of bath soap (not detergent) in 8 quarts/liters of water. Spray. For strong pests, add 2 teaspoons of salt and about 30 mashed cayenne peppers.

Chapter 12 Seeds for Next Year's Garden

With just a little extra effort, we can complete the cycle of nature in our garden by saving our own seeds to plant next year and for many years to come. This will ensure that we have seeds for our favorite varieties available when we want them. And with a good understanding of seed-saving techniques, we can gradually improve the food that we are growing.

OPEN-POLLINATED SEED

To save seed from the plants we grow and have that seed produce healthy plants with the same characteristics as those of the parent plants, we must start with open-pollinated—naturally pollinated, nonhybrid—seeds. Hybrid seeds are usually identified in seed catalogs with the designation F_1.

GENETIC DIVERSITY

Although one plant may be capable of producing much more seed than we need for a small garden, it is important to save seed from at least five plants. Some crops require more than five plants for maintaining genetic diversity; these exceptions are noted in each crop procedure that follows. This minimum number is important for cross-pollinating plants in order to maintain plant vigor and reduce inbreeding, but even for self-pollinating plants, seed from five plants will contain more genetic diversity than seed from one plant.

When genetic diversity is not maintained, plants suffer a loss of health and a decrease in yield from excessive inbreeding, and insect and disease problems are likely to increase. To ensure that the seed you save has adequate genetic diversity, collect seed from at least the number of plants indicated in the crop procedures.

SELF- AND CROSS-POLLINATING

A self-pollinating plant produces flowers that fertilize themselves, and its seeds are likely to produce plants identical to the parent plant. Beans, lettuce, and tomatoes are examples. Cross-pollinating plants, such as carrots and corn, produce flowers that need to be fertilized with pollen from flowers on another plant. This cross-pollination can be carried out by the wind and by insects, especially honeybees. Many self-pollinating plants also benefit from insect activity with improved seed development, so it is important to attract a wide variety of insects to the garden (see chapter 10). When cross-pollinating plants of different varieties exchange pollen, their seeds will produce an unpredictable mixture of plants, and the seed that these plants produce can no longer be considered pure or true-to-type.

WHICH PLANTS

A plant with undesirable qualities should not be used for seed-saving. Plants that look healthy and true-to-type can be marked by tying a colored string around them or on a stick next to them, so that they will not be harvested for food.

You can choose plants that have qualities you wish to encourage: size of fruit, size of plant, color, slowness in going to seed (lettuce, for example), early production (tomatoes and beans, for example).

HOW OFTEN?

If seeds are stored well, you need not save seed from every crop every year. Seed can be kept for several years for planting; the length of time varies for different crops. A seed's ability to germinate and grow is called *viability*. The "Seed-Saving Information" table below gives viability figures for different cops. Use this table to plan how often to save seed from the crops in your garden.

CLEANING

If you are saving seeds for your own garden, it is not necessary for them to be perfectly free of chaff. You can use a screen to sift out small debris. To get rid of larger debris, you can put the seeds on a shallow plate and blow on them gently; or you can pour them from one container to another in a light breeze. For some seeds, you can float off the debris by putting the seeds in a generous amount of water; the debris will float, and you can pour it off. Immediately, strain the water off of the rest of the seeds, which will have sunk to the bottom, and spread them out in a single layer on a paper towel or newspaper to dry in a dry, well-ventilated, warm, shady location as quickly as possible.

STORAGE

Seeds are alive, and keeping them alive and able to germinate and grow well requires good storage conditions. The best conditions for storing seeds are cool and dry. Seeds should be air-dried as thoroughly as possible, then stored in an airtight container.

Glass containers are better than plastic, and wide-mouth canning jars with two-piece lids are the most efficient and convenient.

If you keep the jars in the refrigerator, the life of the seeds will be extended.

GERMINATION

If you are not sure whether your seed has been stored well enough or whether it is too old to use, it is easy to test the germination.

Use two pie pans or plates. Cover one with a double layer of paper towel or newspaper, and moisten the paper thoroughly. Put ten to twenty seeds on the wet surface. Cover the seeds with another double layer of damp paper towel or newspaper, and put the second plate or pie pan upside down over the first plate loosely. Check the paper towel every day to be sure it is moist enough, and add water, if necessary. After four to five days, begin checking to see if the seeds have germinated. When it looks as though no more seeds have germinated, divide the number of germinated seeds by the total number of seeds you used. The result is the germination rate. If your germination rate is low, you can sow more seed to compensate for the ones that may not germinate.

Seed-Saving Information

	1	2	3	4	5	6	7	8	9	10	11
	A/B	V	S/C	SP / NO PL	YR.1	YR. 2	YR. 3	YR. 4	YR. 5	YR. 6	YR. 7
DRY BEANS	A	3	S	4 / 1,343	X				X		
FAVA BEANS	A	2	S	8 / 320	X		X		X		X
SNAP BEANS	A	3	S	4 / 1,343	X			X			X
BUCKWHEAT	A	3	C	4 / 1,343	X			X			X
CARROT	B	3	C	10 / 201	X→			X→			X→
CORN	A	3	C	15 / 84	X		X		X		X
CUCUMBERS	A	5	C	12 / 159	X					X	
GRAINS	A	3	S	5 / 833	X			X			X
LETTUCE	A	6	S	10 / 201	X						X
MELONS	A	6	C	15 / 84	X						X
GREEN ONIONS	B	2	C	6 / 621	X→		X→		X→		X→
REG. ONIONS	B	2	C	6 / 621		X→		X→		X→	
TOMATOES	A	4	S	21 / 35	X	X			X	X	
WATERMELON	A	4	C	22 / 32	X				X		

Column 1: A = annual; B = biennial.

Column 2: V = viability (in years).

Column 3: S = self-pollinating; C = cross-pollinating.

Column 4: Sp/No Pl = spacing (in inches) and number of plants per 100 square feet: This spacing is given in *Booklet 13: Growing to Seed* (see end of this chapter for publication information) as optimal spacing for plants grown for seed. It is also possible to save seed from plants on the spacings recommended elsewhere in this book.

Columns 5-11: Given the characteristics of the different crops, this is a suggested schedule for the years in which to save seeds. Instead of trying to save seeds from almost all of the crops the first year, you could decide to postpone saving some of them until the second or third year.

SELF-POLLINATING ANNUALS

The easiest plants to save seeds from are self-pollinating annuals. Annuals are plants that complete their growth cycle—from planted seed to seed-producing plant—within one growing season.

Tomatoes

Tomato seed is easy to save: We can have our seed and eat our tomato, too! Saving seed from the earliest fruit will encourage the early-producing trait in the tomato seed we save.

For genetic diversity, you should save seed from at least five tomato plants. However, in the bed described in this book, there will probably be enough space for only three tomato plants, so you will need to save seed for two years, making sure that the seed you use for the second year is from the same batch of seed you used for your tomato plants the first year.

To save seed from tomatoes grown from open-pollinated seed, squeeze the tomato seeds and pulp out of ripe tomatoes (harvested from at least five different plants) into a jar and add a little water. Leave the seeds in the jar, uncovered, for about four days, until they begin to ferment—you will see a white mold form on the surface of the water. Pour off the top layer, which contains immature seeds. Pour the seeds remaining at the bottom  of the jar into a strainer, and wash them with clean, cool water. Shake off as much water as possible and spread the seeds out in a single layer on a paper towel or newspaper to dry for several days. Stir them around every day or so, so the clumps of seed do not remain moist. Store in a cool, dry place.

Beans

Beans are easy to save seed from, too. They are easy to harvest and clean and require no extra space or time in the bed. However, for genetic diversity, you will need to save seed from at least seven bean plants. It is best to mark these plants for seed-saving at the beginning of the season. If you eat the first beans, planning to save the later beans for seed, you will be encouraging the late-fruiting trait.

Harvest when the beans are fully mature and the pods are beginning to dry. Spread the pods out in a dry, well-ventilated, shady area, and let them finish drying. As soon as they are completely dry, shell them, and let them dry further. Store them in a cool, dry place.

If you have trouble with weevils getting into your stored bean seeds, you can put the seeds in a well-sealed container after they are thoroughly dry and put the container in the freezer for two days. This will not damage the viability of the seeds. After taking the container out of the freezer, do not open it until it has reached air temperature; if the container is opened before it has reached air temperature, humidity in the air is likely to condense on the seeds, which can greatly reduce their longevity.

Lettuce

Saving lettuce seed involves allowing at least five plants to continue growing past the usual harvest point. When your lettuce is mature and ready to harvest, select the best-looking plants, and mark them with colored string. Let these plants continue to grow until flowers appear at the top of the long stalks. When well over half of the flowers have turned to "fuzz," pull the plant out by the roots and hang it upside down to dry, with the seed heads in a brown paper bag. When the seed heads are thoroughly dry, rub them between your hands to separate the seeds from the chaff. Then clean the chaff from the seed (see p. 94). Store the seeds in a cool, dry place.

Remember to put lettuce seed in the freezer before using it, if the temperature is over 80°F (see p. 60).

Grains

To maintain genetic diversity, you should save seed from at least ten grain plants, rather than five. Otherwise, there are no special instructions for the process of saving seeds from grains; the seed you eat can be planted. See p. 82 for harvesting and cleaning instructions.

It is possible to improve wheat yields by 10 percent per year over a ten-year period by selecting and saving seed from the fullest heads.

Buckwheat

For genetic diversity, seed should be saved from at least fifteen buckwheat plants.

The seeds on buckwheat plants mature at different rates. When it looks as though there are a good number of mature seeds and the plants are approximately 75 percent brown, harvest the plants. You can pull them up or, preferably, cut them at ground level and leave the roots in the soil, especially since buckwheat plants have few roots. Pull off the seed tops and put them somewhere to dry.

When the seed tops are thoroughly dry, rub them between your hands to loosen the seeds. Pour them from one bucket to another several times in a light breeze to clean out the chaff. Seeds cleaned in this way can be planted. For buckwheat seed to be edible, it needs to be dehulled, a process that is difficult to do without special equipment.

CROSS-POLLINATING ANNUALS

Cucumbers, Cantaloupe, and Watermelon

Cucumbers and melons (as well as squash) are cross-pollinated by insects. Melons will not cross with cucumbers, but different varieties of melons (or cucumbers) may cross with each other, so generally, only one variety can be grown for seed in a given season.

Select fruits for seed from at least five different plants, and mark them. Cucumbers will need to stay on the plant at least a month beyond the time when they would be picked to eat, until they have turned yellow. Melon seed is mature when the melon is ready to eat.

To collect the seeds from cucumbers and melons, cut the fruit in half and scrape out the pulp and the seeds with a spoon. Use the same method as for tomatoes (see p. 97). Watermelon seeds do not need this treatment. Just be sure to wash them and dry them thoroughly.

BIENNIALS

Biennial plants produce their edible yield in the first growing season and then need more time to produce their seed. In areas with mild winters, these plants may spend the winter in the garden, but in areas with severe winters, the plants or roots must be stored for the winter, then replanted in the spring for their flower and seed production. Optimal storage conditions include near-freezing, but not below-freezing, temperatures and high humidity, with plants only one layer deep on their sides surrounded by damp sand or damp sawdust.

Onions

Onion flowers can be cross-pollinated by insects, so in a small backyard garden, you should save seed from only one variety in a given year, although you can grow any number of other varieties for eating. If any of the onions you are growing for food happen to go to seed in their first season, do not save seed from them. Going to seed early is not a trait to be encouraged.

Choose the best of your onion crop to replant for seed production. In areas with mild winters, you can plant the selected onions a month or six weeks before your first soft frost. In areas with severe winters, store the onions carefully for the winter, and replant them as soon as the soil can be prepared in the spring. Plant the onions on 6-inch centers, with their necks just at the surface of the soil.

The onion will send up one (usually) or several (sometimes) seed stalks, which will flower and eventually set seed. The seed heads will not mature at the same time, and ripe seed may shatter (disperse on its own), so watch the plants carefully. When the black seeds can be seen, cut off a long piece of stem with the seed head, and put the heads into a large paper bag with plenty of air space around them. Allow them to dry. Rub the seed heads between your hands to loosen the seeds. To get rid of the debris, pour the seeds from one bucket to another several times in a light wind, or use the water method (see p. 95).

Carrots

Carrot flowers are cross-pollinated by insects and can also cross with their wild relative, Queen Anne's lace. Plant carrots to be used for seed so they will be mature in the fall.

Choose large, well-shaped, undamaged carrots with good color. Cut off the tops, one inch from the root. Replant the carrots immediately in areas with mild winters, or store carefully until spring in areas with severe winters. Plant the carrots on 10-inch centers, with the top of the root at or just below the soil surface.

In the spring, the carrot will send up a seed stalk that can grow up to 6 feet tall. Carrot flowers attract a wide variety of beneficial insects. The seeds at the top of the flower stalks will mature first. In a small garden, you can pull up the plants with the roots, put the heads into a brown paper bag, and hang them upside down to dry. When they are thoroughly dry, rub the seed heads between your hands to loosen the seed. Use a screen or other method to clean out the debris.

Corn

In a small garden, it is generally not feasible to save seed from corn properly. At least fifty plants are needed to maintain genetic diversity. If you wish to try saving corn seed, you should read the relevant sections of the books recommended below.

OTHER CROPS

Potatoes

Although occasionally a potato plant will produce a fruit with seeds, potatoes are generally propagated vegetatively—using potatoes from the previous crop. Storing potatoes from the time they have been harvested until the time they are to be planted can be challenging. Diseases can be easily acquired by incorrect storage (see p. 69). The books recommended below can provide more details. Another good source of information is the catalog distributed by Ronniger's Seed & Potato Company (see p. 104 for their address).

RECOMMENDED RESOURCES

The material in this chapter has been simplified in order to make the seed-saving process easier to understand. For more details, see:

Rogers, Marc. *Saving Seeds: The Gardener's Guide to Growing and Storing Vegetable and Flower Seeds.* Williamstown, MA: Storey Communications, 1990.

Donelan, Peter. *Growing to Seed* (Self-Teaching Mini-Series #13). Willits, CA: Ecology Action, 1999 (rev. ed.).

Ashworth, Suzanne. *Seed to Seed: Seed-Saving Techniques for the Vegetable Gardener.* Decorah, IA: Seed Savers Exchange, 1995.

Appendix 1 Supplies and Resources

SEED COMPANY ADDRESSES

Abundant Life Seed Foundation
P.O. Box 772
Port Townsend, WA 98368

W. Atlee Burpee & Co.
300 Park Avenue
Warminster, PA 18991-0001

Garden City Seeds
778 Hwy 93N
Hamilton, MT 59840

Johnny's Selected Seeds
Foss Hill Road
Albion, ME 04910-9731

Nichols Garden Nursery
1190 N. Pacific Hwy.
Albany, OR 97321-4580

Bountiful Gardens
18001 Shafer Ranch Road
Willits, CA 95490

Fisher's Garden Store
P.O. Box 236
Belgrade, MT 59714

J. L. Hudson, Seedsman
Star Route 2, Box 337
La Honda, CA 94020

KUSA Research Foundation
P.O. Box 761
Ojai, CA 93023

Peaceful Valley Farm Supply
P.O. Box 2209
Grass Valley, CA 95945

Peters Seed & Research
P.O. Box 1472
Myrtle Creek, OR 97457

Ronniger's Seed and Potato Co.
P.O. Box 307
Ellensburg, WA 98926

Salt Spring Seeds
P.O. Box 444, Ganges
Salt Spring Island, BC V8K 2W1
Canada

Shepherd's Garden Seeds
30 Irene St.
Torrington, CT 06790-6658

R. H. Shumway's
P.O. Box 1
Graniteville, SC 29829-0001

Stokes Seeds Inc.
Box 548
Buffalo, NY 14240-0548

Vermont Bean Seed Company
Garden Lane
Fair Haven, VT 05743

CATALOGS

In addition to the seed catalogs listed above, we would like to suggest a few others worth browsing through for supplies:

Bountiful Gardens, 18001 Shafer Ranch Road, Willits, CA 95490.
Tools, books, and other useful items.

Peaceful Valley Farm Supply, P.O. Box 2209, Grass Valley, CA 95945.
Tools and supplies for organic farming and gardening.

Walt Nicke's Garden Talk, P.O. Box 433, Topsfield, MA 01983.
Useful products, hints, and articles.

BOOKS

Some of these books may be out of print, but your local library may have them or be able to get them for you through interlibrary loan, or you may be able to find them at a used bookstore.

Vilmorin-Andrieux, M. *The Vegetable Garden*, reprint of 1885 English edition. Berkeley: Ten Speed Press, 1981. Developed by the original French intensive gardeners and added to by their English counterparts. For detailed crop descriptions and growing instructions, some of the best ever written. Beautiful engravings of many varieties.

Park's Success with Seeds. Geo. W. Park Seed Co., 1978, out of print.

Ellis, Barbara W., and Fern M. Bradley, eds.*The Organic Gardener's Handbook of Natural Insect and Disease Control*. Emmaus, PA: Rodale, 1992.

Yepson, Rogert B., ed. *The Encyclopedia of Natural Insect and Disease Control*. Emmaus, PA: Rodale, 1984, out of print.

Hart, Rhonda Massingham. *Bugs, Slugs and Other Thugs: Controlling Garden Pests Organically*. Williamstown, MA: Storey Communications, Inc., 1991.

ECOLOGY ACTION PUBLICATIONS

Jeavons, John. *How to Grow More Vegetables*, 5th ed. Berkeley: Ten Speed Press, 1995. The classic book on Biointensive gardening for both beginners and advanced gardeners. Includes an extensive list of seed companies.

Jeavons, John, J. Mogador Griffin, and Robin Leler. *The Backyard Homestead*. Willits, CA: Ecology Action, 1983. For those who want to develop more self-reliance and who are getting more involved in their food-raising. Includes detailed planning information and plans and instructions for building minigreenhouses.

Duhon, David, and Cindy Gebhard. *One Circle*. Willits, CA: Ecology Action, 1984.

Jeavons, John. *Booklet 14: The Complete 21-Bed Mini-Farm*. Willits, CA: Ecology Action, 1986.

Cox, Carol, and Staff. *Booklet 26: Learning to Grow All Your Own Food*. Willits, CA: Ecology Action, 1991.

Donelan, Peter. *Booklet 13: Growing to Seed*. Willits, CA: Ecology Action, 1999 (rev. ed.).

BIOINTENSIVE-BED STARTER SETS

Here are generous portions of seeds for all the vegetables for your Biointensive bed (except seed potatoes, which can be ordered directly from Ronniger's or purchased from your local nursery), as well as an option for some very helpful tools. The seeds are from Ecology Action's own Bountiful Gardens catalog and are some of the finest varieties available anywhere.

The seeds in this collection are
• Heirloom quality, the kind of seed you would save for your children and grand-children;
• Open-pollinated, so you can save seeds from the crops you grow, if you wish;
• Completely untreated, guaranteed to be fresh, vital, and ready for your garden.

Each of the seed packets contains enough or more than enough seed to plant the area recommended in this book, and complete directions on how, where, and when to plant are included.

Heirloom Garden Vegetable Seed Collection

Derby snap bean	Nantes carrot, Tip Top
Golden Bantam corn	Straight Nine cucumber
Bronze Arrow lettuce	Haogen melon
Rutgers tomato	Southport White Globe onion
Sugar Baby watermelon	White Lisbon onion (green onion)

Compost Crop Seed Collection

Hard red spring wheat

Cereal rye

Banner fava beans

Purple vetch

Calorie Crop Seed Collection

Hard red spring wheat

Taylor's Dwarf Horticultural bean

Hull-less oats

BASIC GARDEN TOOLS

Bountiful Gardens has also put together a collection of tools for the Biointensive gardener.

Redwood seed flat kit. Easy to build! Pre-cut, drilled redwood, nails, and directions for one standard 3-inch-deep flat (14 inches x 23 inches).

Transplanting trowel. Good for moving larger seedlings and for general cultivation. Narrow for better control.

Widger. The British have developed the perfect tool for moving small seedlings. The special shape is ideal.

Haws watering can. A well-balanced tool made of metal or strong, lightweight plastic. The head gives a gentle rain of water.

D-handled spade and fork. Quality wood D-handled spade and fork that stand up well to double-digging.

For current prices for these seed collections, tools, equipment, and other garden supplies and books, write to
Bountiful Gardens
18001 Shafer Ranch Road
Willits, CA 95490,
or telephone (707) 459-6410.

Appendix 2 Additional Tools for Garden Planning

As you get more into gardening, it is a good idea to gather helpful data for your garden site. A rain gauge and a good min/max (minimum/maximum temperature) thermometer from your gardening store will allow you to keep records of precipitation and temperatures. These will enable you to better understand the gardening year.

SOIL

1. Type: _____

(clay, clay-loam, sand, and so on)

2. Soil test report attached

A soil test can be cost-effective if you have five or more beds. We recommend that you have both the basic and the trace mineral analysis done. Our favorite soil-testing service is Timberleaf Soil Testing Service, 39648 Old Spring Road, Murrieta, CA 92563-5566. Write for instructions and a test-sample kit.

3. Age of growing area (how long site has been used for a garden):

_____

4. Size of growing area: _____

Rain gauge

Min/max thermometer

5. Growing area faces: _____ (direction, e.g., SSW)

6. Slope of growing area: _____ (flat, rolling, steep, very steep)

Climate
1. Average monthly minimum/maximum temperatures

January	_____/_____		July	_____/_____
February	_____/_____		August	_____/_____
March	_____/_____		September	_____/_____
April	_____/_____		October	_____/_____
May	_____/_____		November	_____/_____
June	_____/_____		December	_____/_____

2. Average monthly precipitation

January	_____		July	_____
February	_____		August	_____
March	_____		September	_____
April	_____		October	_____
May	_____		November	_____
June	_____		December	_____

KEEPING RECORDS

Make two copies of the forms on the following pages. Use one for precipitation and the other for minimum/maximum temperatures. If you photocopy the forms on 8½-by-11-inch paper, you can put them in a three-ring binder with your other garden records.

Precipitation/Temperatures

JANUARY	FEBRUARY	MARCH
1. _____	1. _____	1. _____
2. _____	2. _____	2. _____
3. _____	3. _____	3. _____
4. _____	4. _____	4. _____
5. _____	5. _____	5. _____
6. _____	6. _____	6. _____
7. _____	7. _____	7. _____
8. _____	8. _____	8. _____
9. _____	9. _____	9. _____
10. _____	10. _____	10. _____
11. _____	11. _____	11. _____
12. _____	12. _____	12. _____
13. _____	13. _____	13. _____
14. _____	14. _____	14. _____
15. _____	15. _____	15. _____
16. _____	16. _____	16. _____
17. _____	17. _____	17. _____
18. _____	18. _____	18. _____
19. _____	19. _____	19. _____
20. _____	20. _____	20. _____
21. _____	21. _____	21. _____
22. _____	22. _____	22. _____
23. _____	23. _____	23. _____
24. _____	24. _____	24. _____
25. _____	25. _____	25. _____
26. _____	26. _____	26. _____
27. _____	27. _____	27. _____
28. _____	28. _____	28. _____
29. _____	29. _____	29. _____
30. _____		30. _____
31. _____		31. _____

APRIL

1. _____
2. _____
3. _____
4. _____
5. _____
6. _____
7. _____
8. _____
9. _____
10. _____
11. _____
12. _____
13. _____
14. _____
15. _____
16. _____
17. _____
18. _____
19. _____
20. _____
21. _____
22. _____
23. _____
24. _____
25. _____
26. _____
27. _____
28. _____
29. _____
30. _____

MAY

1. _____
2. _____
3. _____
4. _____
5. _____
6. _____
7. _____
8. _____
9. _____
10. _____
11. _____
12. _____
13. _____
14. _____
15. _____
16. _____
17. _____
18. _____
19. _____
20. _____
21. _____
22. _____
23. _____
24. _____
25. _____
26. _____
27. _____
28. _____
29. _____
30. _____
31. _____

JUNE

1. _____
2. _____
3. _____
4. _____
5. _____
6. _____
7. _____
8. _____
9. _____
10. _____
11. _____
12. _____
13. _____
14. _____
15. _____
16. _____
17. _____
18. _____
19. _____
20. _____
21. _____
22. _____
23. _____
24. _____
25. _____
26. _____
27. _____
28. _____
29. _____
30. _____

JULY	AUGUST	SEPTEMBER
1.	1.	1.
2.	2.	2.
3.	3.	3.
4.	4.	4.
5.	5.	5.
6.	6.	6.
7.	7.	7.
8.	8.	8.
9.	9.	9.
10.	10.	10.
11.	11.	11.
12.	12.	12.
13.	13.	13.
14.	14.	14.
15.	15.	15.
16.	16.	16.
17.	17.	17.
18.	18.	18.
19.	19.	19.
20.	20.	20.
21.	21.	21.
22.	22.	22.
23.	23.	23.
24.	24.	24.
25.	25.	25.
26.	26.	26.
27.	27.	27.
28.	28.	28.
29.	29.	29.
30.	30.	30.
31.	31.	

OCTOBER	NOVEMBER	DECEMBER
1. _____	1. _____	1. _____
2. _____	2. _____	2. _____
3. _____	3. _____	3. _____
4. _____	4. _____	4. _____
5. _____	5. _____	5. _____
6. _____	6. _____	6. _____
7. _____	7. _____	7. _____
8. _____	8. _____	8. _____
9. _____	9. _____	9. _____
10. _____	10. _____	10. _____
11. _____	11. _____	11. _____
12. _____	12. _____	12. _____
13. _____	13. _____	13. _____
14. _____	14. _____	14. _____
15. _____	15. _____	15. _____
16. _____	16. _____	16. _____
17. _____	17. _____	17. _____
18. _____	18. _____	18. _____
19. _____	19. _____	19. _____
20. _____	20. _____	20. _____
21. _____	21. _____	21. _____
22. _____	22. _____	22. _____
23. _____	23. _____	23. _____
24. _____	24. _____	24. _____
25. _____	25. _____	25. _____
26. _____	26. _____	26. _____
27. _____	27. _____	27. _____
28. _____	28. _____	28. _____
29. _____	29. _____	29. _____
30. _____	30. _____	30. _____
31. _____		31. _____

Index